How the Brain Learns

A Classroom Teacher's Guide

T 80378

Dr. David A. Sousa

ABOUT THE AUTHOR

David A. Sousa is an educational consultant and former superintendent of the New Providence, New Jersey, Public Schools. He has served as a consultant in science and staff development to the New Jersey Department of Education as well as to school districts across the United States and Canada. He is past president of the National Staff Development Council.

He has a bachelor's degree in chemistry from Massachusetts State College at Bridgewater, a Master of Arts in Teaching in science from Harvard University, and a doctorate from Rutgers University in school administration and supervision. He has taught junior and senior high school science, served as a K–12 director of science, and was a K–12 supervisor of instruction and staff development. He is an adjunct professor of education at Seton Hall University and a visiting lecturer at Fairleigh Dickinson and Rutgers Universities.

He has edited science books and published numerous articles in leading journals on staff development, science education, and educational research. He makes his home in New Jersey.

Copyright 1995 by NASSP

ISBN 0-88210-301-6

Published by:
The National Association of Secondary School Principals
1904 Association Drive, Reston, Virginia 22091-1537
Telephone (703) 860-0200; FAX (703) 476-5432

President: *E. Don Brown*
President-Elect: *H. Michael Brown*
Executive Director: *Timothy J. Dyer*
Deputy Executive Director: *Thomas F. Koerner*
Director, Publications and Marketing: *Robert Mahaffey*
Technical Editor and Design: *James Theisen*

Printed in U.S.A.

*Who dares to teach
must never cease to learn.*

— John Cotton Dana

CONTENTS _____

PRACTITIONER'S CORNERS

PREFACE

We are all fully aware that every day administrative, educational, and supervisory challenges can consume significant amounts of educators' time. Knowing how selective your responsibilities require you to be when it comes to making the most effective use of your time, let me assure you that reading this book is well worth your attention.

Dr. David Sousa's *How the Brain Learns* is an educator-oriented compilation of what the last 15 years of paradigm-changing research has discovered about how the human brain works, how our memories seem to operate, and what it all means for our students.

This important work will provide you with insights concerning:

- Effective *teaching* that makes the best use possible of experience, attention span, memory/recall patterns, right/left orientation, and practice.

- Effective *learning* that also makes the best use possible of experience, attention span, memory/recall patterns, right/left orientation, and practice.

An important undercurrent in his book is the realization that if we don't incorporate new and important research about teaching and learning into our daily classroom strategies, we limit our students' opportunities to learn.

Besides exposing myths and stereotypes about learning, the research Sousa describes is so important, its impact so immediate, and its results so demonstrable that his book is virtually indispensable to those who share the goal of providing the most effective learning experiences for all students. His 39 pages of **Practitioner's Corners** blend research and common sense approaches that can help you move closer to realizing that goal for every student.

How the Brain Learns is an important investment in professional growth, and its casual style makes it enjoyable and accessible. Without doubt, principals and teachers will want extra copies to share with colleagues tomorrow.

Sousa's emphasis on the most practical, hands-on techniques provides a powerful springboard for a quantum leap toward more focused teaching, increased student involvement, improved learning, and—so important in these challenging times—optimism and a renewed sense of direction.

Timothy J. Dyer
Executive Director, NASSP

INTRODUCTION _____

You start out as a single cell derived from the coupling of a sperm and egg; this divides into two, then four, then eight, and so on, and at a certain stage there emerges a single cell which will have as all its progeny the human brain. The mere existence of that cell should be one of the great astonishments of the earth.
— Lewis Thomas, *The Medusa and the Snail*

The human brain is an amazing structure—a universe of infinite possibilities and mystery. It constantly shapes and reshapes itself as a result of experience, yet it can take off on its own without input from the outside world. How does it form a human mind, capture experience, or stop time in memory? Although it does not generate enough energy to light a simple bulb, its capabilities make it the most powerful force on Earth.

The New Research

The U.S. scientific community has declared the 1990s "the decade of the brain." Much has been written in recent years about the research that has looked at the workings of the human brain. The more we learn about the brain, the more remarkable it seems. Sophisticated medical instruments are producing new charts of the human brain. Computerized axial tomography (CAT) scanners use focused X-rays to produce detailed cross sections of brain structure. They can detect strokes, cancer, and malformations, but cannot reveal brain functions. A CAT scan cannot distinguish a live brain from a dead one.

Positron-emission tomography (PET) detects radioactively-tagged sugar injected into the patient to track where blood flows in the brain, an indicator for brain activity. When a person sings a song, eats an apple, or recalls a memory, different areas of the brain are activated and recorded by the PET scanner and translated into images. By giving moment-to-moment pictures of the brain during these events, PET scans provide an inside look at how and where the brain activity occurs.

Magnetic resonance imaging (MRI) uses radio waves to disturb the alignment of the body's atoms in a magnetic field. The resulting signals are recorded and formed by a computer. It can record changes in the brain that occur only 50 milliseconds apart and can take a picture of the entire brain once every second. Using both PET and MRI, researchers can determine which parts of the brain are involved in specific tasks and which parts are dormant. Moreover, researchers have discovered a whole family of brain chemicals called neurotransmitters and are investigating their association with various brain functions. To determine what parts of the brain control various functions, neurosurgeons use tiny electrodes to stimulate individual nerve cells and record their reactions. Besides the information collected by these techniques, the growing body of case studies of individuals recovering from various types of brain damage is giving us new evidence about and insights into how the brain develops, changes, learns, and remembers.

Implications for Teaching

As we examine the clues that this research is yielding about learning, we recognize its importance to the teaching profession. Every day teachers enter their classrooms with lesson plans, experience, and the hope that what they are about to present will be understood, remembered, and useful to their students. Yet, the extent that this hope is realized depends largely on the knowledge base that these teachers use in designing those plans and, perhaps more important, on the instructional techniques they select during the lessons.

> *The good news is that the more we discover about how the brain learns, the more successful teaching and learning can be. The bad news is that we cannot get this information to teachers fast enough.*

The good news is that as we discover more about how the brain learns, we can devise strategies that can make the teaching/learning process more efficient, effective, and enjoyable. The bad news is that we cannot get this new information to classroom teachers and other educators fast enough. Although it has been over 15 years since researchers began making major discoveries about how the brain learns, many practicing and prospective classroom teachers are only marginally aware of them. This lack of knowledge about recent brain research affects the quality of our profession's performance and its success in helping others learn.

Why This Book Can Help Improve Teaching and Learning

The purpose of this book is to collect in one place some of the most recent research about the human brain and how it learns, and to suggest strategies that translate the research into effective classroom practices. The strategies are at the end of most chapters in sections called **Practitioner's Corner**. They offer practical suggestions and activities derived from the research that teachers can use to improve the teaching/learning process. This is hardly a novel idea. Madeline Hunter in the late 1960s introduced the notion of teachers using what we are learning about learning and modifying traditional classroom procedures and instructional techniques accordingly. Her program at the UCLA School of Education came to be called "Instructional Theory Into Practice," or ITIP. Readers familiar with that model will recognize some of Dr. Hunter's work here, especially in the areas of transfer and practice. I had the privilege of working periodically with her for nine years, and I firmly believe that she was the major force that awakened educators to the importance of continually updating their knowledge base and focusing on research-based strategies.

This book will help answer questions like:

> When do students remember best in a learning episode?
>
> How can I help students understand and remember more of what I teach?
>
> Why is focus so important?
>
> How can I get students to see meaning in what they are learning?
>
> Why is transfer such a powerful principle of learning, and how can it destroy a lesson without my realizing it?

Principals should find here a substantial source of topics for discussion at faculty meetings which should include, after all, instructional as well as informational items. In doing so, they help foster the attitude that professional growth is an ongoing school responsibility and not an occasional event. More important, being familiar with these topics enhances the principal's credibility as the school's instructional leader and fosters the notion that the school is a learning organization for *all* its occupants.

This book will be useful to **classroom teachers** because it presents a research-based rationale for why and when certain instructional strategies should be used. It focuses on the activities of the brain as the organ of thinking and learning, and takes the approach that the more teachers know about how the brain learns, the more instructional options become available. Increasing the options that teachers have during the dynamic process of instruction also increases the likelihood that successful learning will occur. The book should also help **staff developers** who continually need to update their own knowledge base and include research and research-based strategies and support systems as part of their repertoire. Chapter 7 offers some suggestions to help staff developers implement and maintain the knowledge and strategies suggested here.

The book reflects the state of knowledge about the brain and learning at the time of publication. Since this is an area of intense research, educators need to constantly read about new discoveries and adjust their understandings and strategies accordingly. As the body of research grows, I am more and more convinced that all children can learn if we can discover the ways to teach them.

The ideas in this book will also provide the research support for initiatives such as cooperative learning groups, integrated thematic units, and the interdisciplinary approach to curriculum. Those who are familiar with *constructivism* will recognize many similarities in the ideas presented here. The research is yielding more evidence that knowledge is not only transmitted from the teacher to the learners, but is transformed in the learner's mind as a result of cultural and social mediation. Much of this occurs through elaborative rehearsal and transfer and is discussed in several chapters.

Key thoughts are highlighted in boxes throughout the book.

What Do You Already Know?

The value of this book to you will be measured in part by the degree to which it enhances your understanding of how the brain processes information and learns. One way to discover that enhancement is to take the following true-false test that will help you to assess your current knowledge of brain processing.

Your Current Knowledge of Brain Processing

Directions: Decide whether the following statements are generally true or generally false and circle the appropriate letter.

1.   T   F   The brain acts more like a sponge than a sieve when processing new information.

2.   T   F   Learners who can perform a _new_ learning task well are likely to retain it.

3.   T   F   Reviewing material just before a test is a good indicator of how much has been retained.

4.   T   F   Increased time on task increases retention of new learning.

5.   T   F   The rate at which a learner retrieves information from memory is closely related to intelligence.

6.   T   F   The amount of information a learner can deal with at one time is genetically linked.

7.   T   F   It is usually not possible to increase the amount of information that the working (temporary) memory can deal with at one time.

8.   T   F   Recent research confirms that information in long-term storage deteriorates as we get older.

9.   T   F   Most of the time, the transfer of information from long-term storage is under the conscious control of the learner.

10.   T   F   Intelligence is strongly connected to whether people have left or right brain hemisphere dominance.

11.   T   F   People must be taught how to do higher-order thinking.

The explanations for the answers are identified throughout the book in special boxes. You might be surprised to learn that all the statements are false. How did you do?

CHAPTER 1

BASIC BRAIN FACTS

With our new knowledge of the brain, we are just dimly beginning to realize that we can now understand humans, including ourselves, as never before, and that this is the greatest advance of the century, and quite possibly the most significant in all human history.

— Leslie A. Hart,
Human Brain and Human Learning

Chapter Highlights: This chapter will familiarize you with some of the basic structures of the human brain and their functions. It briefly describes neuron operations and distinguishes between the brain and the mind.

The adult human brain is a wet, fragile mass that weighs a little over three pounds. It is about the size of a small grapefruit and can fit in the palm of your hand. Cradled in the skull and surrounded by protective membranes, it is poised at the top of the spinal column. The brain works ceaselessly, even when we are asleep. Although it represents only about 2 percent of our body weight, it consumes nearly 20 percent of our calories! The more we think, the more calories we burn. Perhaps this can be a new diet fad, and we could modify Descartes' famous quotation from: "I think, therefore I am," to "I think, therefore I'm thin"!

Through the centuries, surveyors of the brain have examined every cerebral feature, sprinkling the landscape with Latin names to describe what they saw. They analyzed structures and functions and sought concepts to explain their observations. One early concept divided the brain by location—forebrain, midbrain, and hindbrain. Another, proposed by Paul MacLean several decades ago, described the brain according to stages of evolution—reptilian, paleomammalian, and mammalian. For our purposes, we will divide the brain into three parts on the basis of their general functions: the cerebrum, the cerebellum, and the brain stem (Figure 1.1).

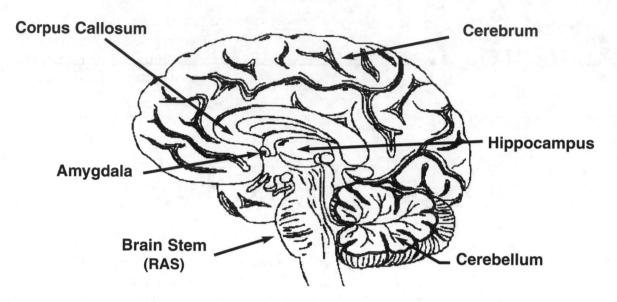

Corpus Callosum

Cerebrum

Hippocampus

Amygdala

Brain Stem
(RAS)

Cerebellum

Figure 1.1. *Cross section of the human brain.*

Cerebrum

A soft jellylike mass, the cerebrum is the largest of the three areas, representing over 80 percent of the brain by weight. Its surface is pale gray, wrinkled, and marked by furrows called fissures. One large fissure runs from front to back and divides the cerebrum into two halves called the cerebral hemispheres. For some still unexplained reason, the nerves from the left side of the body cross over to the right hemisphere, and those from the right side of the body cross to the left hemisphere. The two hemispheres are connected by a thick cable of over 250 million nerve fibers called the corpus callosum. The hemispheres use this bridge to communicate with each other and coordinate activities.

The hemispheres are covered by a thin laminated cortex (meaning bark), rich in cells, that is about one-tenth of an inch thick and has a surface area of about 2.5 square feet. The cortex is composed of six layers of cells meshed in about 10,000 miles of connecting fibers per cubic inch! Scientists have not discovered what occurs in the vast regions below the cortex; they may hold secrets to even more remarkable capabilities of the brain.

Thinking, memory, speech, and muscular movement are controlled by areas in the cerebrum. Deep within the cerebrum lies the limbic system, sometimes called the old brain, that is involved with emotional responses. Its placement between the cerebrum and the brain stem permits the interplay of emotion and reason.

Hippocampus

Located at the base of the cerebrum is the hippocampus (the Greek word for seahorse, because of its shape). It plays a major role in consolidating learning and in converting information from working memory via electrical signals to long-term storage, a process that may take weeks. It constantly checks information relayed to working memory and compares it to stored experiences. This structure is essential for meaning.

Its role was revealed by patients whose hippocampus was damaged or removed because of disease. These patients could remember everything that happened before the operation, but not afterward. If they were introduced to you today, you would be a stranger to them tomorrow. Since they can remember information for only a few minutes, they can read the same article repeatedly and believe on each occasion that it is the first time they have read it.

Amygdala

Attached to the end of the hippocampus is the amygdala (Greek for almond). This almond-shaped structure is part of the limbic system and appears to play an important role in emotions. Electrical stimulation of the amygdala can incite rage. Its surgical removal can turn a raging epileptic into a docile individual. Stimulation does not always produce rage; it can also cause fear or pleasure. Because of its proximity to the hippocampus and its activity on PET scans, researchers believe that the amygdala encodes an emotional message, if one is present, when learning is transferred from working memory to long-term storage. The emotional message is recalled whenever the memory is recalled. This explains why people recalling an emotional memory will often experience those emotions again. Researchers in cognitive science are beginning to understand the important role that emotions play in cognitive learning. This emotion-cognitive connection will be discussed in later chapters.

Cerebellum

The cerebellum ("little brain") is located just below the rear part of the cerebrum. It is the area that coordinates every movement. Although it initiates nothing on its own, the cerebellum monitors impulses from nerve endings in the muscles. It modifies and coordinates commands to swing a golf club, smooth a dancer's footsteps, and allow a hand to bring a cup to the lips without spilling its contents. The cerebellum may also store the memory of rote movements, such as touch-typing and tying a shoelace. A person whose cerebellum is damaged cannot coordinate movement, catch a ball, or complete a handshake.

Brain Stem

The third part is the brain stem, the oldest and deepest part of the brain, that evolved 500 million years ago. It is often referred to as the reptilian brain since it resembles the entire brain of a reptile. Of the 12 body nerves that go to the brain, 11 end in the brain stem (the olfactory nerve goes directly to the cerebrum, an evolutionary artifact). Here is the center of sensory reception and where vital body functions, such as heartbeat, respiration, body temperature, and digestion are monitored and controlled. The brain stem also houses the reticular activating system, or perceptual register, about which more will be explained in the next chapter.

Brain Cells

The brain is composed of a trillion cells of at least two known types, nerve cells and glial cells. The nerve cells are called *neurons*. The glial (meaning "glue") cells are support cells that hold the neurons together and act as filters to keep harmful substances out of the neurons.

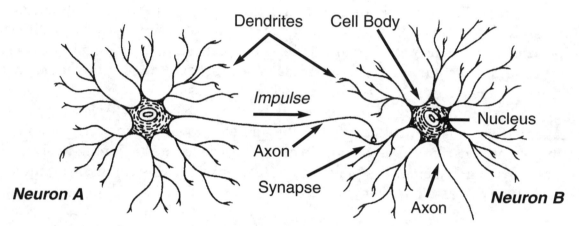

Figure 1.2. Neurons, or nerve cells, transmit impulses along an axon and across the synapse to the dendrites of the neighboring cell.

The neurons are the functioning core for the brain and the entire nervous system. The body of each neuron is about 1/100th the size of the period at the end of this sentence. Unlike other cells, the neuron (see Figure 1.2) has tens of thousands of branches emerging from its core called *dendrites* (from the Greek word for tree). The dendrites receive electrical impulses from other neurons and transmit them along a long fiber called the *axon*. There is normally only one axon per neuron.

A layer called the myelin sheath surrounds each axon. The sheath insulates the axon from the other cells and increases the speed of impulse transmission. This impulse travels along the neurons through an electrochemical process and can move the entire length of a six-foot adult in two-tenths of a second. A neuron can transmit between 250 and 2,500 impulses per second.

Neurons have no direct contact with each other. Between each dendrite and axon is a small gap of about a millionth of an inch called a synapse (from the Greek, "to join together"). A typical neuron collects signals from others through the dendrites, which are covered at the synapse with thousands of tiny bumps called spines. The neuron sends out spikes of electrical activity (impulses) through the axon to the synapse where the activity releases chemicals stored in sacs at the end of the axon. These chemicals, called neurotransmitters, either excite or inhibit the neighboring neuron. Over 50 different neurotransmitters have been discovered so far. Learning occurs by changing the synapses so that the influence of one neuron on another also changes.

The proportion of glial cells to neurons may play a role in how well one thinks. Examinations of Albert Einstein's brain tissue show many more glial cells per neuron than average. Could these additional support cells account for the way he could think of extraordinary things that our senses could not even imagine?

There also seems to be a direct connection between the physical world of the brain and the work of the brain's owner. Recent studies of neurons in people of different occupations show that the more complex the skills demanded of the occupation, the more dendrites were found on the neurons. This increase in dendrites allows for more connections between neurons resulting in more sites to store learnings.

There are about 100 billion neurons in the adult human brain—about 20 times as many neurons as people on this planet, and about 10 times the number of stars in the Milky Way. Each neuron has tens of thousands of dendrite branches. While it is impossible to calculate the number of combinations of synapse pathways that can be formed in one brain, they are conservatively estimated at over 100 times the total atoms in the universe! (Ornstein and Thompson, 1984)

The number of potential pathways in just one human brain is estimated at over 100 times the total number of atoms in the universe!

This inconceivably large number allows the brain to process the data coming continuously from the senses, to store decades of memories, faces and places, to learn languages, and to combine information in a way that no other individual on this planet has ever thought of before. A remarkable achievement for three pounds of soft tissue!

Neuron Development in Children

The neurons in a child's brain make many more connections than those in adults. A newborn's brain makes connections at an incredible pace as the child absorbs its environment. The richer the environment, the greater the number of interconnections that are made, and learning can take place faster and with greater meaning. As the child approaches puberty, the pace slackens and two other processes begin: Connections the brain finds useful become permanent; those not useful are eliminated—the brain is selectively strengthening and pruning connections based on experience. This process continues throughout our lives, but it appears to be at its greatest between the ages of 2 and 11. Thus, at an early age, experiences are already shaping the brain and designing the neural architecture that will influence how it handles future experiences in school, work, and other places.

The Brain and the Mind

I do not equate the brain and the mind. In my view, they are separate entities. The brain is the physical organ composed of atoms and molecules that inhabits the skull. The mind is much more than that; it transcends the head and operates throughout the body. Of course, they are linked and intertwined. Every few years nearly every atom in the brain (and the rest of the body as well) is replaced. Yet one's persona, memories, hopes, and dreams remain unchanged and survive this complete makeover of the physical self.

The qualities of the mind include the ability to be aware of itself, to understand its place on the planet and in time, and its capacity to use language for abstract representations. The mind puts meaning and purpose into our lives and gives us a world view. It has no boundaries and permeates every cell of our body. While this book will deal primarily with brain function and learning, I cannot ignore the realization that the mind can do many more things that no one can explain … at least, not yet.[1]

---

1. Those interested in pursuing the brain-mind connection should consult works such as J. A. Hobson, *The Chemistry of Conscious States: How the Brain Changes its Mind* (Boston, Mass.: Little, Brown, 1994) and E. Harth, *The Creative Loop: How the Brain Makes a Mind* (Reading, Mass.: Addison-Wesley, 1993).

CHAPTER 2 _____

HOW THE BRAIN
PROCESSES INFORMATION

*There are probably more differences in human brains than
in any other animal partly because the human brain does
most of its developing in the outside world.*
— Robert Ornstein and Richard Thompson,
The Amazing Brain

Chapter Highlights: This chapter presents a modern dynamic model of
how the brain deals with information from the senses. It covers the behavior of the two temporary memories, the criteria for long-term storage, and the impact of the self-concept on learning.

While the brain remains largely a mystery beyond its own understanding, we
are slowly uncovering more about its baffling processes. Using MRI and PET
scans, researchers can display in vivid color the differences in brain cell metabolism that occur in response to different types of brain work. Based on the level of ra-
dioactivity in different parts of the brain, a computer constructs a color-coded map indicating what different areas are doing during such activities as learning new words, analyzing tones, doing mathematical calculations, or responding to images. One thing is
clear: The brain calls selected areas into play depending on what the individual is doing
at the moment. This knowledge encourages us to construct models that explain data and
behavior, but models are useful only when they contain some predictability about specific operations.

The Information Processing Model

Several models exist to explain brain behavior. In designing a model for this book, I
needed one that would accurately represent the complex research of neuroscientists in

such a way as to be understood by educational practitioners. I recognize that a model is just one person's view of reality, and I readily admit that this particular information processing model comes closest to my view of how the brain learns. It differs from other models in that it escapes the limits of the computer metaphor and recognizes that learning, storing, and remembering are dynamic and interactive processes. Beyond that, the model incorporates much of the recent findings of research and is sufficiently flexible to adjust to new findings as they are revealed. I have already made several changes in this model since I began working with it nearly 10 years ago. My hope is that presenting it to classroom teachers may encourage them to reflect on their methodology and decide if there are new insights here that could affect their instruction and improve learning.

Origins of the Model

The precursor of this model was developed by Robert Stahl of Arizona State University in the 1980s. Stahl's more complex model synthesized the research in the 1960s and 1970s on cognitive processing and learning. His goal was to convince teacher educators that they should use this model to help prospective teachers understand how and why learning occurs. He also used the model to develop an elaborate and fascinating learning taxonomy designed to promote higher-order thinking skills.

Usefulness of the Model

The model discussed here (Figure 2.1) is a significantly modified version of Stahl's original. It has been updated and streamlined so that it can be used by the widest range of teacher educators and practitioners. It uses common objects to represent various stages in the process. Even this revised model does not pretend to include all the ways that researchers believe the human brain deals with information, thought, and behavior. It limits its scope to the major cerebral operations that deal with the collecting, evaluating, storing, and retrieving of information—the parts most useful to educators.

The model starts with information from our environment and shows how the senses reject or accept it for further processing. It then explains the two temporary memories, how they operate, and the factors that determine if a learning will be stored or not. Finally, it shows the inescapable impact that experiences and self-concept have on future learning. The model is simple, but the processes are extraordinarily complex. Knowing how the human brain seems to process information and learn can help teachers plan lessons that students are more likely to understand and remember.

Limitations of the Model

Although the explanation of the model will follow items going through the processing system, it is important to note that this linear approach is used solely for simplicity and clarity. Much of the recent evidence on memory supports a model of parallel processing. That is, many items are processed quickly and simultaneously (within limits), taking different paths through and out of the system. Memories are dynamic and dispersed, and the brain has the capacity to change its properties as the result of experience.

While the model may seem to represent learning and remembering as a mechanistic process, it must be remembered that we are describing a *biological process*. Nonetheless, I have avoided a detailed discussion of the biochemical changes that occur within and between neurons since that would not contribute to the understanding necessary to convert the fruits of this research and this model into successful classroom practices, which is, after all, the goal of this book.

Inadequacy of the Computer Model

The rapid proliferation of computers has encouraged the use of the computer model to explain brain functions. This is indeed tempting. Using the analogy of input, processing, and output seems so natural, but there are serious problems with this model. Certainly, the smallest hand-held calculator can out-tally the human brain in solving complex mathematical operations. Larger computers can play chess, translate one language into another, and correct massive manuscripts for spelling and grammatical errors in just seconds. The brain performs slower because of synaptic delays, the time it takes for a nerve impulse to travel along the axon, and because the capacity of working memory is limited. But computers cannot exercise judgment with the ease of the human brain. Even the most sophisticated computers are closed linear systems limited to binary code, the 0s and 1s in linear sequences that are the language of computer operations.

The human brain has no such limitations. It is an open, parallel-processing system continually interacting with the physical and social worlds outside. It analyzes, integrates, and synthesizes information and abstracts generalities from it. It can recognize a face in less than a second—something no computer can do. According to Russell (1979), the entire world's telephone system is equivalent to only one gram of the human brain —a piece the size of a pea! Each neuron is alive and altered by its experiences and its environment. As you read these words, neurons are interacting with each other, reforming and dissolving storage sites, and establishing different electrical patterns that correspond to your new learning. For these and many other reasons, the computer model is woefully inadequate and misleading.

The Model and Constructivism

At first glance, the model may seem to perpetuate the traditional approach to teaching and learning—that students repeat newly learned information in quizzes, tests, and reports. On the contrary, the new research is revealing that students are more likely to gain greater understanding of and derive greater pleasure from learning when allowed to *transform* the learning into creative thoughts and products. This model emphasizes the power of transfer during learning and the importance of moving students through higher levels of complexity of thought. This will be explained further in Chapter 4.

The Senses

Our brain takes in more information from our environment in a single day than the largest computer does in years. That information is detected by our five senses. The senses do not contribute equally to our learning. Over the course of our lives, sight, hearing and touch contribute to about 95 percent of all new learning.

> **About 95 percent of all new learning during our lifetime is through sight, hearing, and touch.**

Our senses constantly collect bits of information from the environment, even while we sleep. These bits average 40,000 per second![2] This may seem very high, but think about it. The nerve endings all over your skin are detecting the clothes you are wearing. Your ears are hearing sounds around you, the rods and cones in your eyes are picking up this print as they move across the page, you may still be tasting recent food or drink, and your nose may be detecting an odor. Put these bits of data together and it is easy to see how they can add up. Of course, the stimuli must be strong enough for the senses to record them.

The 40,000 bits of data per second is an average count over the course of a day. This number will be higher if you are deeply involved in a multi-sensory learning experience and lower if you are in an unstimulating environment.

Perceptual Register

Imagine if the brain had to give its full attention to all those bits of data at once; we would blow the cerebral equivalent of a fuse! Fortunately, the brain has evolved a structure that screens all these data to determine the importance to the individual. This structure is commonly called the *perceptual* or *sensory register*. The technical name for it is the *reticular activation system* (RAS) and it is located in the brain stem (Figure 1.1). The perceptual register is drawn in the model as the side view of slats, as in Venetian blinds; the reason will become clear later.

The perceptual register monitors the strength and nature of the sensory impulses and, in just milliseconds (a millisecond is one-thousandth of a second), uses the individual's experience to determine the data's degree of importance. Most of the data signals are unimportant, so the perceptual register blocks them and they drop out of the processing system. Have you ever noticed how you can be in a room studying while there is construction noise outside? Eventually, it seems that you no longer hear the noise.

Your perceptual register is blocking these repetitive stimuli, allowing your conscious brain to focus on more important things. This process is called *perceptual filtering* and we are largely consciously unaware of it. One form of autism is believed to occur when an

---

2. The numbers used in this chapter are averages over time. There are always exceptions to these values as a result of human variations or pathologies.

Information Processing Model

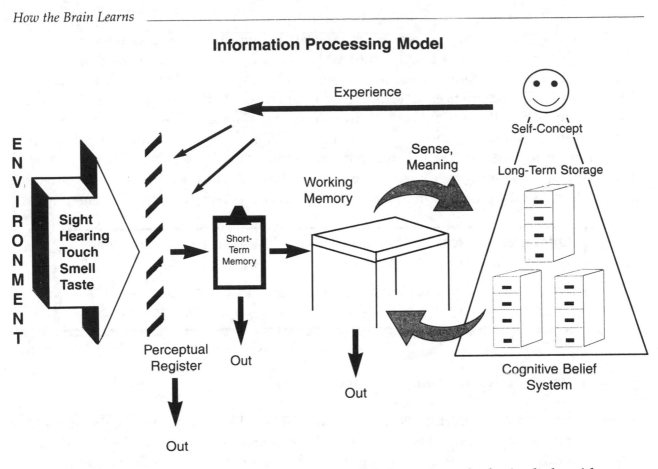

Figure 2.1. The Information Processing Model shows how the brain deals with information from the environment. (Adaptation and enhancement of original model by Robert Stahl.)

individual is unable to filter sensory information. This sensory overload is like living inside a pinball machine, and the brain responds by blocking *all* of it.

Short-Term Memory

If the sensory data are important, or if the perceptual register becomes overloaded, the data are passed on to the first of two temporary memories, called *short-term memory*. If you took a psychology course more than a decade ago, you learned that we had two memories—one short-term (temporary) memory and one long-term (permanent) memory. The idea that we seem to have two temporary memories is recent. It is a way of explaining how the perceptual register deals with an overload of sensory data, and how we can continue to process sensory stimuli subconsciously for many seconds beyond the perceptual register's time limits.

These two temporary memories are called short-term memory, which acts simply as an extension of the perceptual register, and *working memory*, where conscious processing occurs. When older literature refers to short-term memory, it really means working memory and not the short-term memory described here.

The short-term memory area is represented in the model as a clipboard, a place where we put information briefly until we make a decision on how to dispose of it. Short-term memory operates subconsciously and holds data for up to about 30 seconds. The individual's experiences determine its importance. If the datum is of little or no importance within this time frame, it drops out of the system. For example, when you look up the telephone number of the local pizza parlor, you usually can remember it just long enough to make the call. After that, the number is of no further importance and drops out of short-term memory. (Note that we have already two major places where information can drop out within just a few seconds of its reception by the senses.)

> **Test Question No. I**: The brain acts more like a sponge than a sieve when processing new information.
>
> **Answer**: False. The brain acts more like a sieve because there are several early stages where most data are dropped from the system.

Examples of Short-Term Memory at Work

Here are two other examples to understand how the processing occurs up to this point. Suppose you decide to wear a new pair of shoes to work today. They are snug, so when you put them on, the receptors in your skin send impulses to the perceptual register. For a short time you feel discomfort. After a while, however, as you get involved with work, you do not notice the discomfort signals anymore. The perceptual register is now blocking the impulses from reaching your consciousness. Should you move your foot in a way that causes the shoe to pinch, however, the perceptual register will pass this pain stimulus along to your consciousness and you become aware of it.

Another example: You are sitting in a classroom and a police car with its siren wailing passes by. Experience recalls that a siren is an important sound. It signals the perceptual register to pass these auditory data immediately over to short-term memory. If over the next few seconds the sound of the siren gets fainter, experience signals the short-term memory that the sound is of no further importance and the auditory data are blocked and dropped from the system. All this is happening subconsciously while your attention is focused on something else. If asked about the sound later, you will not remember it. You cannot recall what you have not stored.

Suppose, on the other hand, that the siren sound gets louder and suddenly stops, followed by another siren that gets louder and stops. Experience will now signal that the sounds are important because they are nearby and require your attention. At this point, the now-important auditory data move rapidly through short-term memory and into working memory for conscious processing.

Threats and Emotions Affect Memory Processing

This last example illustrates another characteristic of brain processing: There is a hierarchy of response to sensory input (Figure 2.2). Any input that is of higher priority diminishes the processing of data of lower priority. Thus, data interpreted as posing a threat to the survival of the individual, such as a burning odor, a snarling dog, or someone threatening bodily injury, are processed immediately.

Emotional data also take high priority. When an individual responds emotionally to a situation, the older limbic system (stimulated by the amygdala) takes a major role and the complex cerebral processes are suspended. We have all had experiences when anger, fear of the unknown, or joy quickly overcame our rational thoughts. This override of conscious thought can be strong enough to cause temporary inability to talk ("I was dumbfounded") or move ("I froze"). This happens because the hippocampus is susceptible to stress hormones which can inhibit cognitive functioning and long-term memory. Hart (1983) called this process *downshifting*. Under certain conditions, emotions can enhance memory by causing the release of hormones that stimulate the amygdala to signal brain regions to strengthen memory. Strong emotions can shut down conscious processing during the event while enhancing our memory of it.[3] Emotion is a powerful and misunderstood force in learning and memory.

> **Threats and emotions inhibit cognitive processing.**

Working Memory

Working memory is the second temporary memory and the place where conscious, rather than subconscious, processing occurs.[4] The information processing model represents working memory as a work table, a place of limited capacity where we can build, take apart, or rework ideas for eventual storage somewhere else. When something is in working memory, it generally captures our focus and demands our attention.

Capacity

Working memory can handle only a few items at once. This functional capacity changes with age. The table on p. 15 shows how the capacity of working memory increases as one passes through the major growth spurts in cognitive development.[5]

---

3. For more on this phenomenon, see the work of Larry Squires, University of California at San Diego. A summary of his research appeared in *The New York Times*, October 25, 1994, pp. C1 and C11.

4. The older literature calls this area short-term memory. The two terms for the same area will cause confusion until they become standardized in newer writings.

5. For the original research on working memory capacity, see the work of George A. Miller in his article, "The Magical Number Seven, Plus or Minus Two: Some Limits in Our Capacity for Processing Information," *Psychological Review*, 63: 81–97.

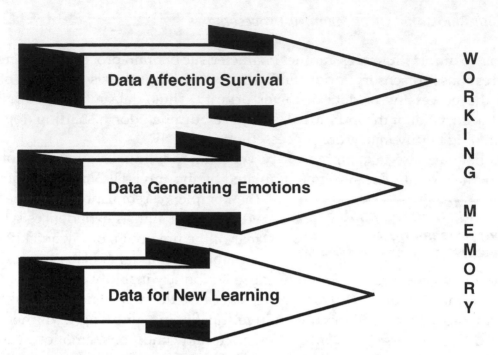

**W
O
R
K
I
N
G

M
E
M
O
R
Y**

Figure 2.2. Data for survival and data that generate emotions are processed ahead of data for new learning.

Pre-school infants can deal with about two items of information at once. Pre-adolescents can handle three to seven items, with an average of five. Through adolescence, further cognitive expansion occurs and the capacity range increases to five to nine, with an average of seven. For most people, that number is constant throughout their lives.

Let's test this notion. Get a pencil and a piece of paper. When ready, stare at the number below for seven seconds, then look away and write it down. Ready? Go.

9217053

Check the number you wrote down. Chances are you got it right. Let's try it again with the same rules. Stare at the number below for seven seconds, then look away and write it down. Ready? Go.

4915082637

Again, check the number you wrote down. Did you get all 10 of the digits in the correct sequence? Probably not. Since the digits were random, you had to treat each digit as a single item, and your working memory just ran out of functional capacity.

This limited capacity explains why we have to memorize a song or a poem in stages. We start with the first group of lines by repeating them frequently. Then we memorize the next lines and repeat them with the first group, and so on. It is possible to increase the number of items within the functional capacity of working memory through a process called chunking. This process will be explained in the next chapter.

CHANGES IN CAPACITY OF WORKING MEMORY WITH AGE			
Approximate Age Range in Years	Capacity of Working Memory in Number of Items		
	Minimum	Maximum	Average
Less than 5	1	3	2
Between 5 and 14	3	7	5
14 and Older	5	9	7

Time Limits

Working memory is temporary and can deal with items for only a limited time. How long is that time? This intriguing question has been clinically investigated for over a century, starting with the work of Hermann Ebbinghaus (1850–1909) during the 1880s. He concluded that we can process items intently in working memory (he called it short-term memory) for up to 45 minutes before becoming fatigued. Because Ebbinghaus mainly used himself as the subject to measure retention in laboratory conditions, the results are not readily transferable to the average high school classroom.

Russell (1979) shows this time span to be much shorter and age dependent. For pre-adolescents, it is more likely to be 5 to 10 minutes, and 10 to 20 minutes for adolescents and adults. These are average times and it is important to understand what the numbers mean. An adolescent (or adult) normally can process an item in working memory intently for 10 to 20 minutes before fatigue or boredom with that item occurs and the individual's focus drifts. For focus to continue, there must be some change in the way the individual is dealing with the item. For example, the individual may switch from thinking about it to physically using it, or making different connections to other learnings. If something else is not done with the item, it is likely to drop from the working memory.

This is not to say that some items cannot remain in working memory for hours, or perhaps days. Sometimes we have an item that remains unresolved—a question whose answer we seek or a troublesome family or work decision that must be made. These items can remain in working memory, continually commanding some attention and, if of sufficient importance, interfere with our accurate processing of other information.

Criteria for Long-Term Storage

Now comes the most important decision of all: Should the items in working memory move to long-term storage for future recall, or should they drop out of the system? This is an important decision because we cannot recall what we have not stored. Yet teachers teach with the hope that students will retain the learning objective for future use. So, if the learner is ever to recall this information in the future, it has to be stored.

What criteria does the working memory use to make that decision? It seems that the learner's working memory asks just two questions to determine whether an item is saved or rejected. They are: "Does this make *sense*?" and "Does this have *meaning*?" Imagine the many hours that go into planning and teaching lessons, and it all comes to these two questions! Let's review them.

"Does this make sense?" This question refers to whether the learner can understand the item based on experience. Does it "fit" into what the learner knows about how the world works? When a student says, "I don't understand," it means the student is having a problem making sense of the learning.

> **Sense and meaning are usually required for new learning to be stored.**

"Does it have meaning?" This question refers to whether the item is *relevant* to the learner. For what purpose should the learner remember it? Meaning, of course, is a very personal thing and is greatly influenced by our experiences. The same item can have great meaning for one student and none for another. When a student asks, "Why do I have to know this?" it indicates the student has not, for whatever reason, accepted this learning as relevant.

Here are two examples to explain the difference between sense and meaning. Suppose I tell a 15-year-old student that the minimum age for getting a driver's license in his state is 16, but is 17 in a neighboring state. He can understand this information, so it satisfies the sense criterion. But the age in his own state is much more relevant to him, since this is where he will apply for his license. Chances are high that he will remember his own state's minimum age (it has both sense *and* meaning) but will forget that of the neighboring state since it has sense but lacks meaning.

Suppose you are a teacher and you read in the newspaper that the average salary for dock workers last year was $52,000, while the average for teachers was $38,000. Both numbers make sense to you, but the average teacher's salary has more meaning since you are in that profession.

Whenever the learner's working memory decides that an item does not make sense or have meaning, the probability of it being stored is extremely low (see Figure 2.3). If either sense or meaning is present, the probability of storage increases significantly. If both sense *and* meaning are present, the likelihood of storage is very high.

Relationship of Sense to Meaning

Sense and meaning are independent of each other. Thus, it is possible to remember an item because it makes sense but has no meaning. If you have ever played *Trivial Pursuit*, you may have been surprised at some of the answers you knew. If another player asked how you knew that answer, you may have replied, "I don't know. It was just there!" This happens to all of us. During our lifetime, we pick up bits of information that made sense at the time and, although they were trivial and had no meaning, they made their way into our long-term storage. Some neuropsychologists estimate that up to 10 percent of what we have in long-term storage may have been acquired in this manner.

It is also possible to remember an item that makes no sense but has meaning. My sixth-grade teacher once asked the class to memorize the nonsense poem from Lewis Carroll's *Jabberwocky*. It begins, *Twas brillig, and the slithy toves did gyre and gimble in the wabe.* The poem made no sense to us sixth graders, but when the teacher said that she would call on each of us the next day to recite it before the class, it suddenly had meaning. Since I didn't want to make a fool of myself in front of my peers, I memorized it and recited it correctly the next day, even though I had no idea what the sense of it was.

Meaning Is More Significant

Of the two criteria, meaning has the greater impact on the probability that information will be stored. Think of all the television programs you have watched that are NOT stored, even though you spent one or two hours with the program. The show's content or story line made sense to you, but if meaning was absent, you just did not save it. It was entertainment and no learning resulted from it. You might have remembered a summary of the show or whether it was enjoyable or boring, but not the details. On the other hand, if the story reminded you of a personal experience, then meaning was present and you were more likely to remember some details of the program.

Now think of this process in the classroom. Every day, students listen to things that make sense but lack meaning. They may diligently follow the teacher's instructions to perform a task repeatedly, and may even get the correct answers, but if they have not found meaning after the learning episode, there is little likelihood of long-term storage. Mathematics teachers are often frustrated by this. They see students using a certain formula to solve problems correctly one day, but they cannot remember how to do it the next day. If the process was not stored, the information is treated as brand new again!

Sometimes, when students ask why they need to know something, the teacher's response is, "Because it's going to be on the test." This response adds little meaning to a learning. Students resort to writing the learning in a notebook so that it is preserved in writing, but not in memory. We wonder the next day why they forgot the lesson.

For the most part, teachers spend the major portion of their planning and instructional time dealing with how to help students make sense of the lesson objective, and devote little time to making it meaningful. Yet, shifting more classroom emphasis to meaning is likely to increase retention of learning. Some suggestions on how to enhance meaning are found in Chapter 3.

Test Question No. 2: *Learners who can perform a new learning task well are likely to retain it.*

Answer: *False. We cannot presume that because a learner performs a new learning well, it will be permanently stored. Sense and meaning must be present to some degree for storage to occur.*

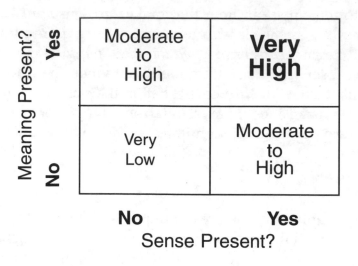

Figure 2.3. *The probability of storing information varies with the degree of meaning and sense present.*

Test Question No. 3: *Reviewing material just before a test is a good indicator of how much has been retained.*

Answer: *False. Reviewing material just before a test allows students to enter the material into working memory for immediate use. Thus, this procedure cannot verify that what the learner recalls during the test was from long-term storage.*

Long-Term Storage

Storing occurs when the hippocampus encodes information and sends it to one or more long-term storage areas. The encoding process takes time. While learners may *seem* to have acquired the new information or skill in a lesson, there is no guarantee that there will be permanent storage after the lesson. How do we know if retention has occurred? If the student can accurately recall the learning after a sufficient period of time has passed, we say that the learning has been retained. Since research on retention shows that the greatest loss of newly-acquired information or a skill occurs within 18–24 hours, the 24-hour period is a reasonable guideline for determining if information was transferred into long-term storage. If a learner cannot recall new learning after 24 hours, there is a high probability that it was not stored and, thus, can never be recalled.[6]

---

6. This point has implications for how we test students for retention of previously-learned material. See the **Practitioner's Corner** at the end of this chapter on how to test whether information is in long-term storage.

Sometimes, we store the "gist" of an experience, not the specifics. This may occur after watching a movie. We store a generalization about the plot, but few, if any, details.

The long-term storage areas are represented in the model as file cabinets—places where information is kept in some type of order. While there are three file cabinets in the diagram for simplicity, we do not know how many long-term storage sites actually are in the brain. Researchers such as Steven Rose (1992) demonstrate that long-term memory is a dynamic, interactive system that activates storage areas distributed across the brain to retrieve and construct memories. We will discuss this more in the next chapter.

Long-Term Memory and Long-Term Storage

This is a good place to explain the difference between the terms *long-term memory* and *long-term storage*. As used here, long-term memory refers to the process of storing and retrieving information. Long-term storage refers to where in the brain the memories are kept. Think of the long-term storage sites as a library and of long-term memory as a librarian who retrieves information and returns it to its proper storage places.

The Cognitive Belief System

The total of all that is in our long-term storage areas forms the basis for our view of the world around us. This information helps us to make sense out of events, to understand the laws of nature, to recognize cause and effect, and to form decisions about goodness, truth, and beauty. This total construct of how we see the world is called the *cognitive belief system*. It is shown in the information processing model as a large triangle extending beyond the long-term storage areas (file cabinets). It is drawn this way to remind us that the thoughts and understandings that arise from the long-term storage data are greater than the sum of the individual items. In other words, one marvelous quality of the human brain is its ability to combine individual items in many different ways. As we accumulate more items, the number of possible combinations grows geometrically.

Since no two of us have the same data in our long-term storage (not even identical twins raised in the same environment have identical data sets), no two of us see the world in exactly the same way. There are many different ways that people can put the same data together. To be sure, there are areas of agreement: Gravity, for example (few rational people would dispute its effects), or inertia, since most people have experienced the lurch forward or backward when a moving vehicle rapidly changes speed.

> **The cognitive belief system is our view of the world around us and how it works.**

There can be strong disagreement, however, about what makes an object or person beautiful, or an act justified. The persistent debates over abortion and capital punishment are testimony to the wide range of perspectives that people have over any issue. These differences reflect the ways individuals use the experiences in their long-term storage areas to interpret the world around them.

Here is a simple example of how experiences can interpret the same information differently. Suppose I ask you to form the mental image of an "old bat." What picture comes to mind? For some baseball fans, it might be a marred wooden club that has seen too many games. A zoologist, however, might picture an aging fruit bat as it flies haltingly among the trees. Still others might recall an old hag whose complaining made their lives unpleasant. Here are at least three very different images generated by the same two words, each one formed by individuals whose experiences are different from the others.

Self-Concept

Deep within the cognitive belief system lies the *self-concept*. While the cognitive belief system portrays the way we see the world, the self-concept describes the way we view *ourselves* in that world. I might conceptualize myself as a good softball player, an above-average student, or a poor mathematician. These and a long list of other descriptions form part of a person's self-concept.

The self-concept is represented in the model as a face and is placed at the apex of the triangle to emphasize its importance. Self-concept is used here as a neutral term that can run the gamut from very positive to very negative (Figure 2.5). The face on the diagram has a smile, indicating a positive self-concept, but for some people, the face might have a frown since they may not see themselves as positive beings in their world. Emotions play an important role in forming a person's self-concept.

Self-Concept and Experiences

Our self-concept is shaped by our experiences. Some of our experiences, such as passing a difficult test or getting recognition for a job well-done, raised our self-concept. Other experiences, such as getting a reprimand or failing to accomplish a task, lowered our self-concept. These experiences produced strong emotional reactions that the brain's amygdala encoded and stored with the cognitive event. These emotional cues are so strong that we often re-experience the emotion each time we recall the event.

Accepting or Rejecting New Learning

Remember that the perceptual register and short-term memory use experience as the criterion for determining the importance of incoming data to the individual. Thus, if an individual is in a new learning situation and experience signals the perceptual register and short-term memory that prior encounters with this information were successful, then the information is very likely to pass along to working memory. The learner now consciously recognizes that there were successes with this information and focuses on it for further processing. But if experiences produced failure, then the self-concept signals the perceptual register to block the incoming data, just as Venetian blinds are closed to block light. The learner resists being part of the unwanted learning experience and re-

How the Brain Learns

Self-Concept

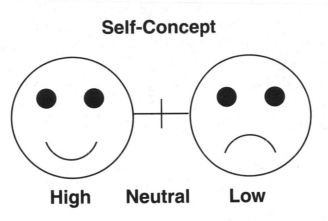

High   Neutral   Low

Figure 2.5. Self-concept describes how we see ourselves in the world. It can range from very high to very low and vary with different learning situations.

sorts to some other cerebral activity, internal or external, to avoid the situation. In effect, the learner's self-concept has closed off the receptivity to the new information. As mentioned earlier in discussing the hierarchy of data processing, when a concept struggles with an emotion, the emotion almost always wins. Of course, it is possible for reason to override emotions, but that takes time and conscious effort.

Let us use an example to explain this important phenomenon. Someone who was a very successful student in mathematics remembers how that success boosted self-concept. As a result, the individual now feels confident when faced with basic mathematical problems. On the other hand, if this person was a poor mathematics student, the lack of success lowered the self-concept. Consequently, the individual will avoid dealing with mathematical problems whenever possible. People will participate in learning activities that have yielded success for them and avoid those that have produced failure.

Dealing with Self-Concept

Students who experience this self-concept shutdown in the classroom often give signals of their withdrawal—folding their arms, losing themselves in other work, or causing distraction. Too often, teachers deal

> **Self-concept can greatly affect how an individual responds to a new learning situation.**

with this withdrawal by reteaching the material, usually slower and louder. But they are attacking the problem from the front end of the information processing system, and this is rarely successful. It is the equivalent of putting a brighter light outside the closed Venetian blinds, hoping the light will penetrate. If the blinds are fully closed and effective, no light will get through, regardless of how bright it may be.

The better intervention is to deal with the learner's emotions that are affecting the self-concept, that is, to convince the learner to allow the perceptual register to open the

21

blinds and pass the learning along. But since the self-concept controls the blinds, the learner must believe that participating in the learning will produce new successes rather than repeat past failures. When teachers provide these successes, they encourage students to open the perceptual register and, ultimately, to participate and achieve in the once-avoided learning. In short, the self-concept is an important participant in controlling the feedback loop and in determining how the individual will respond to almost any new learning. Recognizing this connection gives teachers new insight on how to deal with reluctant learners.

This completes our trip through the information processing model. Remember that the brain is a parallel processor and deals with many items simultaneously. While it rejects much data, it stores some. The next chapter will examine the nature of memory and the factors that determine and help in the retention of learning.

PRACTITIONER'S CORNER

Sensory Preferences and Learning Style

Although we use all five senses to collect information from our environment, they do not contribute equally to our knowledge base. Most people do not use sight, hearing, and touch equally during learning. Just as most people develop a left or right-handed preference, they develop preferences for certain senses as they gather information from their environment.

Some people have a preference for learning by sight. They are called *visual* learners. Others who use hearing as the preferred sense are known as *auditory* learners. Still others who prefer touch or whole-body involvement in their learning are called *kinesthetic* learners. Sensory (also called *modality*) preferences are an important component of an individual's learning style. Teachers need to:

- **Understand** that students with different sensory preferences will behave differently during learning, and

- **Recognize That They Tend To Teach the Way They Learn.** A teacher who is a strong auditory learner will prefer this modality when teaching. Students who also are strong auditory learners will feel comfortable with this teacher's methods, but visual learners will have difficulty in maintaining focus. They will doodle or look at other materials to satisfy their visual craving.

- **Note**, similarly, that students with auditory preferences will want to talk about their learning and will become frustrated with teachers who use primarily visual strategies. Strong kinesthetic learners require movement while learning or they become restless—tapping their pencils or feet, squirming in their seats, or finding reasons to walk around the room.

- **Avoid** misinterpreting these variations in learning style behavior as inattention or as intentional misbehavior. They may, in fact, represent the natural responses of learners with different and strong preferences.

- **Understand** that teachers' own learning styles and sensory preferences can affect learning and teaching. They should design lessons that include activities to address all preference styles.

PRACTITIONER'S CORNER

Developing a Classroom Climate Conducive to Learning

Nearly all learning that occurs in schools involves complex cerebral processing. This occurs more easily in environments free from threat or intimidation. Whenever a student detects a threat, the cerebrum downshifts and thoughtful processing gives way to emotion or survival reactions. Experienced teachers have seen this in the classroom. Under pressure to give a quick response, the student begins to stumble, stabs at answers, gets frustrated, angry, and may even resort to violence.

There are ways to deal with questions and answers that reduce the fear of giving a wrong answer. The teacher could:

• Supply the question to which the wrong answer belongs: "You would be right if I had asked ... "

• Give the student a prompt that leads to the correct answer.

• Ask another student to help.

Threats to students loom continuously in the classroom. The teacher's capacity to humiliate, embarrass, reject, and punish all constitute perceived threats to students. Many students even see grading more as a punitive than as a rewarding process. Students perceive threats in varying degrees, but the presence of a threat in *any* significant degree impedes learning. One's thinking and learning functions operate fully only when one feels secure.

Teachers can make their classrooms better learning environments by avoiding threats (even subtle intimidation) and by establishing democratic climates in which students are treated fairly and feel free to express their opinions during discussions. In these environments students:

• Develop trust in the teacher

• Exhibit more positive behaviors

• Are less likely to be disruptive

• Show greater support for school policy

• Sense that thinking is encouraged and nurtured.

PRACTITIONER'S CORNER

Increasing Processing Time Through Motivation

Motivational factors can increase the time that working memory deals with information. Wlodkowski and Jaynes (1990) and Hunter (1982) suggest a few that teachers can use:

- **Generate Interest**. If the learner is interested in the item, then the processing time can be extended significantly because the learner is dealing with the item in different ways and making new connections with past learnings that once were also of interest. The working memory is seeking ways to use this new learning to enhance the usefulness of the past learning. We all know students who won't give us five minutes of their undivided attention in class, but who spend hours working on a stamp collection or repairing a carburetor.

  Teachers can identify these interests by having their students complete interest inventories at the beginning of the school year. The information gathered from these surveys can help teachers design lessons that include references to student interests as often as possible. Guidance counselors have more information on the types and sources of interest inventories.

- **Establish Accountability**. When learners believe they will be held accountable for new learning, processing time increases. High school students have little difficulty staying on task in driver education classes. Not only do they have interest, but they know they will be legally accountable for their knowledge and skills long after they complete the license tests.

- **Provide Feedback**. When students get prompt, specific, and corrective feedback on the results of their thinking, they are more likely to continue processing, making corrections, and persisting until successful completion. Many brief quizzes that are carefully corrected and returned promptly are much more valuable learning tools than the unit test, and are much more likely to help students be more successful. This success will improve self-concept and encourage them to try more difficult tasks. Computers are motivating because they provide immediate and objective feedback and allow students to evaluate their progress and understand their level of competence.

PRACTITIONER'S CORNER

Increasing Processing Time Through Motivation – Continued

Another effective strategy suggested by Hunter (1982) for increasing process-ing time through motivation is called *level of concern*. This refers to how much the student cares about the learning. We used to think that if the students had anxi-ety about learning, then little or no learning occurred, but there is helpful anxiety (desire to do well) and there is harmful anxiety (threats). Having anxiety about your job performance will usually get you to put forth more effort to obtain pos-itive results. When you are concerned about being more effective (helpful anxi-ety), you are likely to learn and try new strategies.

Students also need a certain level of concern to stimulate their efforts to learn. When there is no concern, there is little or no learning. If there is too much con-cern, anxiety shuts down the learning process and emotions take over. The teach-er then has to seek the level of concern that produces the optimum processing time and learning. Hunter offers four ways to raise or lower the level of concern in a learning situation.

- **Consequences**. Teachers raise the level of concern when they say "This is going to be on the test" and lower it with "Knowing this will help you learn the next set of skills more easily."

- **Visibility**. Standing next to a student who is off task will raise that stu-dent's concern; moving away from an anxious student will lower it. Telling students their work will be displayed can also raise concern.

- **Amount of Time**. Giving students only a little time to complete a learn-ing task will raise concern; extending the time will lower it.

- **Amount of Help**. If there is little or no help available to students while completing a learning task, concern rises. On the other hand, if they have quick access to help, concern lowers. This can be a problem. If stu-dents can always get immediate help to solve a problem, they may be-come dependent and never learn to solve it for themselves. There comes a time when the teacher needs to reduce the help and tell the stu-dents to use what they have learned to solve the problem on their own.

PRACTITIONER'S CORNER

Creating Meaning in New Learning

Meaning refers to the relevancy that students attach to new learning. Meaning isn't inherent in content, but rather the result of how the students relate it to their past learnings and experiences. Questions like "Why do I need to know this?" reveal a learner who is having difficulty determining the relevancy of the new topic. Here are a few ways teachers can help students attach meaning to new learning.

- **Modeling**. Models are examples of the new learning that the learner can perceive in the classroom rather than relying on experience. Models can be concrete (a model of an engine) or symbolic (a map). To be effective, a model should:

  - Accurately and unambiguously highlight the critical attribute(s) of new learning. A dog is a better example of a mammal than a whale.

  - Be given first by the teacher to ensure that it is correct during this period of prime time when retention is highest.

  - Avoid controversial issues that can evoke strong emotions and redirect the learner's attention.

- **Examples from Students' Experience**. Examples from students' experiences allow them to bring previous knowledge into working memory to accelerate making sense and attaching meaning to the new learning. Make sure that the example is clearly relevant to the new learning. This is not easy to do on the spot, so examples should be thought out in advance when planning the lesson.

- **Creating Artificial Meaning**. When it is not possible to identify elements from student experience for examples, we can resort to other devices to develop meaning. Mnemonic devices are ways to associate material so students can remember it. Examples are HOMES to remember the Great Lakes, and "Every good boy does fine" for the musical notes *e, g, b, d,* and *f.* (See Chapter 3.)

PRACTITIONER'S CORNER

Using Closure To Enhance Sense and Meaning

Closure describes the covert process whereby the learner's working memory summarizes for itself its perception of what has been learned. It is during closure that a student often completes the rehearsal process and attaches sense and meaning to the new learning, thereby increasing the probability that it will be retained in long-term storage.

- **Initiating Closure**: To initiate closure, the teacher gives directions that focus the student on the new learning, such as "I'm going to give you about two minutes to think of the three causes of the Civil War that we learned today; be prepared to discuss them briefly." In this statement, the teacher is providing adequate quiet time for the cerebral summarizing to occur and has included a following overt activity (discussion) for student accountability. During the discussion, the teacher can assess the quality and accuracy of what occurred during closure and make any necessary adjustments in teaching.

- **Closure is Different from Review**. In review, the teacher does most of the work, repeating key concepts that were made during the lesson and re-checking student understanding. In closure, the student does most of the work by mentally rehearsing and summarizing those concepts and deciding whether they make sense and have meaning.

- **When to Use Closure**. The teacher can use closure at various times in a lesson.

  It can start a lesson: "Think of the two causes of the Civil War we talked about yesterday and be prepared to discuss them."

  It can occur during the lesson (called *procedural closure*) when the teacher moves from one sub-learning to the next: "Review those two rules in your mind before we learn the third rule."

  It should also take place at the end of the lesson (called *terminal closure*) to tie all the sub-learnings together.

Taking time for closure is an investment that can pay off dramatically in increased retention, thereby furthering student understanding and achievement.

PRACTITIONER'S CORNER

Testing Whether Information Is in Long-Term Storage

Information that the learner processes during a lesson remains in working memory where it eventually will be dropped out or saved for long-term storage. Stahl (1985) notes that just because students *act* as if they have learned the new information or skill doesn't mean it will be transferred to long-term storage at the end of the lesson. Extensive research on retention indicates that 70–90 percent of new learning is forgotten 18–24 hours after the lesson. Consequently, if the new learning survives this time period intact, it is probably in long-term storage and will not deteriorate further.

This time requirement confirms that the processing and transfer between working memory and long-term storage needs adequate time for the encoding and consolidation of the new information into the storage networks. Thus, tomorrow is the earliest reliable time we can confirm that what was learned today has been indeed retained.

How To Test. If teachers want to test whether information actually has been transferred to long-term storage, what type of test should they give? Using what we know about retention, the test:

- Should be given no sooner than 24 hours after the learning.

- Should test on precisely what should have been retained.

- Should come as a surprise to the learner, with no warning or preparation time.

Rationale. If the learners have warning about the test, they are likely to review the material just before the test. In this case, the test may determine the amount of information the learners were able to cram and hold in working memory and *not* what they have recalled from long-term storage. While testing without warning may seem insensitive, it is the only way teachers can be sure that long-term storage was the source of the test information that the learners provided. Unannounced quizzes, then, should help students assess what they have remembered, rather than be a classroom management device to get students back on task.

PRACTITIONER'S CORNER

Testing Whether Information Is in Long-Term Storage – Continued

Misuse of Tests. Some teachers use unannounced tests as punishment to get students back on task. This is a misuse of a valuable tool. Teachers should:

- **Establish** sense and meaning to increase the probability that retention will occur.

- **Explain** to students that unannounced tests or quizzes help them see what as well as how much they have retained and learned over a given period of time.

- **Ensure** that the test or quiz matches the rehearsal when it was first taught. If the learning required essentially rote rehearsal, give a rote type of test. If it required elaborate rehearsal, use a test that allows the students more flexibility in their responses.

Using the Test Results. It is important that teachers:

- **Analyze** immediately the results of the test to determine what areas need to be untaught or practiced. If some students forgot parts, consider forming cooperative learning groups that focus on reteaching the forgotten areas.

- **Decide** whether memory strategies such as concept maps, mnemonics, or chunking (see following chapters) can help in retention.

The analysis might also reveal areas of the curriculum that might need to be reworked or updated for relevance or it might show that the lesson should be retaught in a different way. A task analysis on a failed lesson is a good way to detect false assumptions about learning that the teacher may have made, and it recasts the lesson into a new presentation that can be more successful for both students and teacher.

Using tests as tools to help students to be right, rather than to catch them being wrong, will create a supportive learning climate that results in improved student performance.

CHAPTER 3

MEMORY, RETENTION, AND LEARNING

The multimedia of modern memory devices free us of the necessity to remember vast areas of facts and processes, liberating, presumably, great numbers of neurons and their synapses to other purposes.

— Stephen Rose, *The Making of Memory*

Chapter Highlights: This chapter probes the nature of memory. It explains why our ability to retain information varies within a learning episode and with the teaching method used. It also discusses the value and dangers of practice and techniques for increasing the capacity of working memory.

Memory Makes Us Unique

Memory gives us a past and a record of who we are and is essential to human individuality. Without memory, life would be a series of meaningless encounters that have no link to the past and no use for the future. Memory allows individuals to draw on experience and use the power of prediction to decide how they will respond to future events.

For all practical purposes, the capacity of the brain to store information is unlimited. That is, with about 100 billion neurons, each with thousands of dendrites, the brain will hardly run out of space to store all that an individual learns in a lifetime.[7] Learning is the

---

7. This poses an interesting question: Why is there so much space if we will never fill it? One theory holds that primitive humans needed to make many decisions each day for their survival. Therefore, solving critical problems daily using higher-order thinking resulted in the evolution of a highly-developed cerebrum.

process by which we acquire new knowledge and skills; memory is the process by which we retain the knowledge and skills for the future. Most of what we have in the cognitive belief system, we have learned. Investigations into the neural mechanisms required for different types of learning are revealing more about the interactions between learning new information, memory, and changes in brain structure. As muscles improve with exercise, the brain seems to improve with use. While learning does not increase the number of brain cells, it does increase their size, their branches, and their ability to form more complex networks.

The brain goes through physical and chemical changes when it stores new information as the result of learning. Storing gives rise to new neural pathways and strengthens existing pathways. Thus, every time we learn something, our long-term storage areas undergo anatomical changes that, together with our unique genetic makeup, constitute the expression of our individuality.

How Memory Forms

What is a memory? Is it actually located in a piece of the brain at a specific spot? Are memories permanent? How does the brain manage to store a lifetime of memories in an organ the size of a melon? The definitive mechanism for memory is still elusive. Nevertheless, neuroscientists have discovered numerous mechanisms that occur in the brain that, taken together, define a workable hypothesis about memory formation.

The Memory Trace

You will recall from Chapter 1 that nerve impulses travel down the axon to the gap, or synapse, where neurotransmitter chemicals are released (Figure 3.1). These chemicals cross the synapse to the dendrite of the other neuron. The dendrites are covered with little bumps, called spines, that contain chemical receptor sites. As the chemical messages enter the spines, they may spark a series of electrochemical reactions that cause this second neuron to generate a signal or "fire." The

> **The brain goes through physical and chemical changes each time it learns.**

reaction causes more receptor sites to form on the spines. The next time neurotransmitters cross that particular synapse, the spines will take in more of these chemicals and the stimulation will be stronger, ultimately forming a new memory trace, or *engram*. These individual traces associate and form networks so that whenever one is triggered, the whole network is strengthened, thereby consolidating the memory and making it more easily retrievable.

Memories are not stored intact. Instead, they are stored in pieces and distributed in sites throughout the cerebrum. The shape, color, and smell of an orange, for example, are categorized and stored in different sets of neurons. Activating these sites simultaneously brings together a recollection of our thoughts and experiences involving an orange. Exactly how this happens is still a mystery.

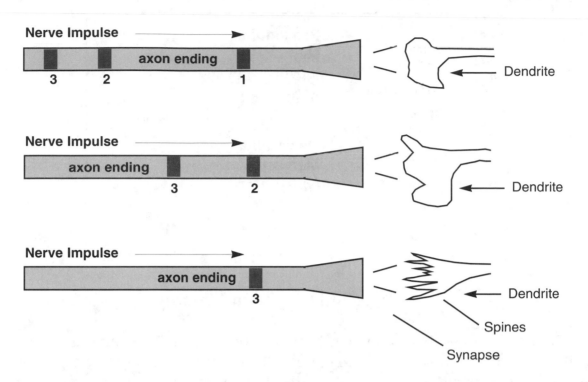

Figure 3.1. A memory trace is formed when repeated stimulation of the same neural pathway by nerve impulses causes the spines to form more receptors for neurotransmitters.

There is also some evidence that the brain stores an extended experience in more than one network. Which sites to select for storage could be determined by the number of associations that the brain makes between the new learning and past learnings. The more connections that are made, the more understanding and meaning the learner can attach to the new learning, and the more likely it is that it will be stored in different networks. This process now gives the learner multiple opportunities to retrieve the new learning.

Persistence in Working and Long-Term Memories

When the signal repetitions along the axon are few, then the spines formed at the affected synapses are too few and too small to associate. This, then, results in an essentially electrochemical reaction and may explain why information in working memory usually does not persist longer than a few hours. If there are many repetitions of the impulse traveling along the neural pathway (through rehearsal and practice), then many larger spines are formed so that there are anatomical changes at the synapses and the memory trace persists.

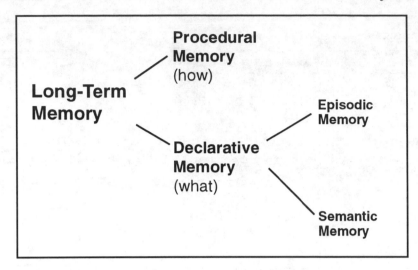

Types of Long-Term Memory

Attempting to use the observable behaviors of memory to identify different types is a difficult task. Neuroscientists are not in total agreement with psychologists as to the characteristics, including time, that clearly describe the different aspects of long-term memory. Nonetheless, there is considerable agreement on some types, and their description is important to understand before setting out to design learning activities.

Procedural memory refers to remembering *how* to do something, like riding a bicycle, driving a car, swinging a golf club, and tying a shoelace. As practice of the skills continues, these memories become more efficient and can be performed with little conscious thought or recall. Procedural memories are processed primarily by the cerebellum.

Declarative memory describes the remembering of names and objects, as in where I live and the kind of car I own, and are processed by the hippocampus and cerebrum.

We seem to store these types of memories differently. Studies (Rose, 1992) of brain-damaged and amnesia victims show that they may still be perfectly capable of riding a bicycle (procedural) without remembering the name, bicycle, or when they learned to ride (declarative). Procedural and declarative memory seem to be stored in different regions of the brain, and declarative memory can be lost while procedural is spared.

Declarative memory can be further divided into episodic and semantic. Episodic memory refers to the memory of events in one's own life history, while semantic memory is knowledge of facts and data that is independent of that history. A veteran knowing that there was a Vietnam War in the 1970s is semantic memory; remembering his experiences in that war is episodic memory.

How the learner processes new information has a great impact on the quality of what is learned and is a major factor in determining whether and how it will be retained. Memories, of course, are more than just information. They represent fluctuating patterns of associations and connections across the brain from which the individual extracts order and meaning. Studies of memory reveal intriguing patterns that suggest strategies teachers and learners can use to improve the retention and retrieval of learning.

Retention of Learning

Retention refers to the process whereby long-term memory preserves a learning in such a way that it can locate, identify, and retrieve it accurately in the future. As explained earlier, this is an inexact process influenced by many factors, including the length and type of rehearsal that occurred, the critical attributes that may have been identified, the student's learning style, and, of course, the influence of prior learnings.

The information processing model in Chapter 2 identifies some of these factors and sets the stage for finding ways to transfer what we know into daily classroom practice. Let us look more specifically at the way the brain processes and retains information during a learning episode, how the nature of that processing affects the degree of retention, and how the degree of retention varies with the length of the episode.

Rehearsal

The assignment of sense and meaning to new learning can occur only if the learner has adequate time to process and reprocess it. This continuing reprocessing is called rehearsal and is a critical component in the transference of information from working memory to long-term storage. The concept of rehearsal is not new. Even the Greek scholars of 400 BC knew its value. They wrote:

> *Repeat again what you hear; for by often hearing and saying the same things, what you have learned comes complete into your memory.*
>
> — from the *Dialexeis*

Two major factors should be considered in evaluating rehearsal: The amount of time devoted to it, which determines whether there is both initial and secondary rehearsal, and the type of rehearsal carried out, which can be rote or elaborative.

Time for Initial and Secondary Rehearsal

Time is a critical component of rehearsal. Initial rehearsal occurs when the information first enters working memory. If the learner cannot attach sense or meaning, and if there is no time for further processing, then the new information is likely to be lost. Providing sufficient time to go beyond the initial processing to secondary rehearsal allows the learner to review the information, to make sense of it, to elaborate on the details, and to assign value and relevance, thus increasing significantly the chance of long-term storage. When done at the end of a learning episode, this rehearsal is called closure.

Students carry out initial and secondary rehearsal at different rates of speed and in different ways, depending on the type of information in the new learning and their learning styles. As the learning task changes, learners automatically shift to different patterns of rehearsal.

Rote and Elaborative Rehearsal

Rote Rehearsal. This type of rehearsal is used when the learner needs to remember and store information exactly as it is entered into working memory. This is not a complex strategy, but it is necessary to learn information or a skill in a specific form or sequence. We use rote rehearsal to remember a poem, the lyrics and melody of a song, multiplication tables, telephone numbers, and steps in a procedure.

Elaborative Rehearsal. This type of rehearsal is used when it is not necessary to store information exactly as learned, but when it is more important to associate the new learnings with prior learnings to detect relationships. This is a more complex thinking process in that the learner reprocesses the information several times to make connections

> **There is almost no long-term retention without rehearsal.**

to previous learnings and assign meaning. Students use rote rehearsal to memorize a poem, but elaborative rehearsal to interpret its message. When students get very little time for, or training in, elaborative rehearsal, they resort more frequently to rote rehearsal for nearly all processing. Consequently, they fail to make the associations or discover the relationships that only elaborative rehearsal can provide. Also, they continue to believe that learning is merely the recalling of information as learned rather than its value for generating new ideas, concepts, and solutions.

> **Test Question No. 4**: *Increased time on task increases retention of new learning.*
>
> **Answer**: *False. Simply increasing a student's time on a learning task does not guarantee retention if the student is not allowed the time and help to personally interact with the content through rehearsal.*

When deciding on how to use rehearsal in a lesson, teachers need to consider the time available as well as the type of rehearsal appropriate for the specific learning objective. Keep in mind that rehearsal only contributes to, but does not guarantee that information will transfer into long-term storage. But there is almost no long-term retention *without* rehearsal.

Retention During a Learning Episode

When an individual is processing new information, the amount of information retained depends, among other things, on when it is presented during the learning episode. At certain time intervals during the learning we will remember more than at other intervals. Try a simple activity that Madeline Hunter devised to illustrate this point. You will need a pencil and a timer. Set the timer to go off in 12 seconds. When you start the timer, look at the list of 10 words on the next page. When the timer sounds, cover the list and write as many of the 10 words as you remember on the lines to the right of the list. Write each word on the line that represents its position on the list, i.e., the first word on line one, etc. Thus, if you cannot remember the eighth word, but you remember the ninth, write it on line number nine.

Ready? Start the timer and stare at the word list for 12 seconds. Now cover the list and write the words you remember on the lines to the right. Don't worry if you did not remember all the words. Turn to your list again and circle the words that were correct. To be correct, they must be spelled correctly and be in the proper position on the list. Look at the circled words. Chances are you remembered the first 3–5 words (lines 1 through 5) and the last 1–2 words (lines 9 and 10), but had difficulty with the middle words (lines 6–8). Read on to find out why.

KEF	1. _____
LAK	2. _____
MIL	3. _____
NIR	4. _____
VEK	5. _____
LUN	6. _____
NEM	7. _____
BEB	8. _____
SAR	9. _____
FIF	10. _____

Primacy-Recency Effect

Your pattern in remembering the word list is a common phenomenon and is referred to as the primacy-recency effect. In a learning episode, we tend to remember best that which comes first, and remember second best that which comes last. We tend to remember least that which comes just past the middle of the episode. This is not a new discovery. Ebbinghaus published the first studies on this phenomenon in the 1880s.

The information processing model in Chapter 2 helps to explain this phenomenon. The first items of new information are within the working memory's functional capacity, command our attention, and are likely to be retained. The later information, however, exceeds the capacity and is dropped. As the learning episode concludes, items in working memory are sorted or chunked to allow for additional processing of the arriving final items.

Figure 3.2 shows how the primacy-recency effect influences retention during a 40-minute learning episode.[8] The times are approximate and averages. Note that it is a bimodal curve, each mode representing the degree of greatest retention during that time

8. Many of the original studies used for these graphs can be found in E. J. Thomas, "The Variation of Memory with Time for Information Appearing During a Lecture," *Studies in Adult Education*, April 1972, pp. 57–62.

period. For future reference, I will label the first or primary mode *prime-time-1*, and the second or recency mode *prime-time-2*. Between these two modes is the time period in which retention during the lesson is least. I will refer to that area as the *down-time*. This is not a time when no retention takes place, but a time when it is more difficult for retention to occur.

> **During a learning episode, we remember best that which comes first, second best that which comes last, and least that which comes just past the middle.**

Implications for Teaching

Teach New Material First

There are important implications of the primacy-recency effect for teaching a lesson. The learning episode begins when the learner focuses on the teacher with intent to learn. New information or skills should be taught first, during prime-time-1, since it is most likely to be remembered. Keep in mind that the students will remember almost any information coming forth at this time. It is important, then, that only correct information be presented. This is not the time to be searching for what students may know about something. I remember watching a teacher of English start a class with, "Today, we are

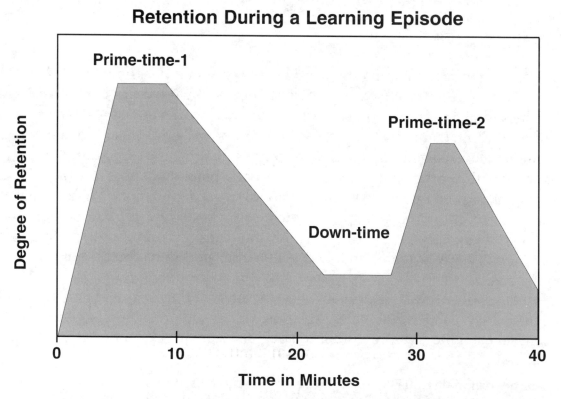

Figure 3.2. The degree of retention varies during a learning episode.

going to learn about onomatopoeia. Does anyone have an idea what that is?" After several wrong guesses, he finally defined it. Regrettably, those same wrong guesses appeared in the follow-up test. And why not? They were mentioned during the most powerful retention position, prime-time-1.

The new information or skill being taught should be followed by practice or review during the down-time. At this point, the information is no longer new and the practice helps the learner organize it for further processing. Closure should take place during prime-time-2, since this is the second most powerful learning position and an important opportunity for the learner to determine sense and meaning.

> **When you have the students' focus, teach the new information. Don't let prime time get contaminated with wrong information.**

Adding these activities to the graph in Figure 3.3 shows how we can take advantage of research on retention to design a more effective lesson.

Misuse of Prime Time

Even with the best of intentions, teachers with little knowledge of the primacy-recency effect can do the following: After getting focus by telling the class the day's lesson objective, the teacher takes attendance, distributes the previous day's homework, collects

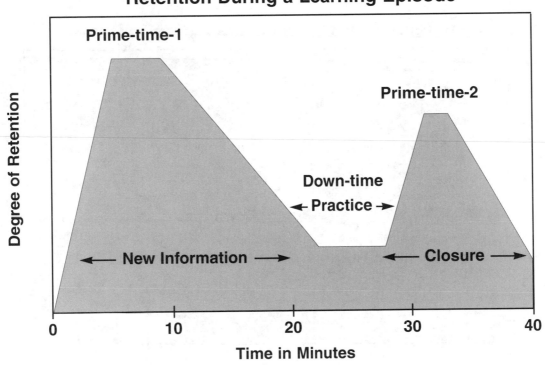

Retention During a Learning Episode

Figure 3.3. *New information and closure are best presented during the prime-time periods. Practice is appropriate for the down-time segment.*

that day's homework, requests notes from students who were absent, and reads an announcement about a club meeting after school. By the time the teacher gets to the new learning, the students are already at the down-time. As a finale, the teacher tells the students that they were so well-behaved during the lesson that they can do anything they want during the last five minutes of class (that is, during prime-time-2) as long as they are quiet. I have observed this scenario, and I can attest that the next day those students remembered who was absent and why, which club met after school, and what they did at the end of the period. The new learning, however, was difficult to remember because it was presented at the time of least retention.

Retention Varies with Length of Teaching Episode

Another fascinating characteristic of the primacy-recency effect is that the proportion of prime-times to down-time changes with the length of the teaching episode. Look at Figure 3.4 below. Note that during a 40-minute lesson, the two prime-times total about 30 minutes, or 75 percent of the teaching time. The down-time is about 10 minutes, or 25 percent of the lesson time. If we double the length of the learning episode to 80 minutes (Figure 3.5), the down-time increases to 30 minutes or 38 percent of the total time period. As the lesson time lengthens, the percentage of down-time increases faster than for prime-time. The information is entering working memory faster than it can be sorted or checked, and accumulates. This cluttering interferes with the sorting and chunking pro-

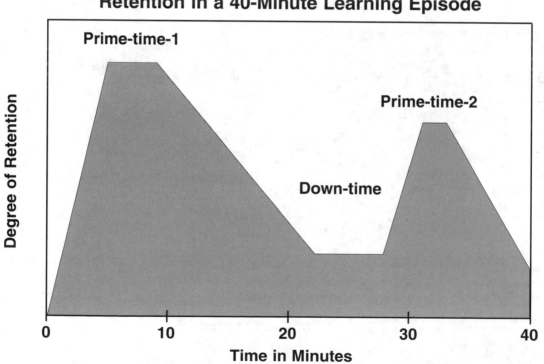

Figure 3.4. Degree of retention during a 40-minute lesson.

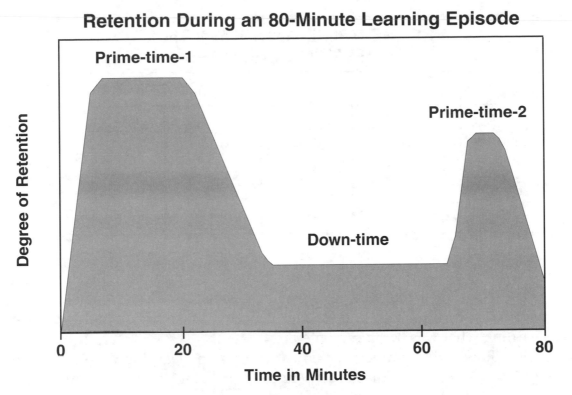

Figure 3.5. Degree of retention during an 80-minute lesson.

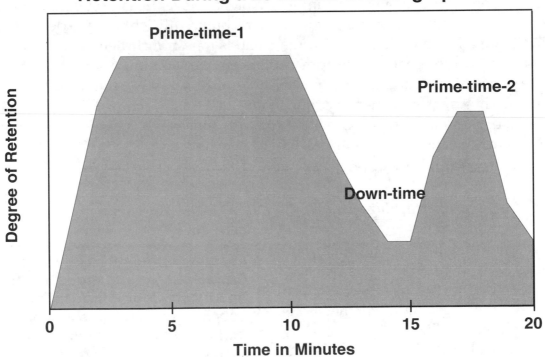

Figure 3.6. Degree of retention during a 20-minute lesson.

AVERAGE PRIME AND DOWN-TIMES IN LEARNING EPISODES				
	Prime-Times		Down-Time	
Episode Time	Total Number of Minutes	Percent of Total Time	Number of Minutes	Percent of Total Time
20 min.	18	90	2	10
40 min.	30	75	10	25
80 min.	50	62	30	38

cesses and reduces the learner's ability to attach sense and meaning, thereby decreasing retention. Think back to some of those college classes that lasted for two hours. After the first 20 minutes or so, didn't you find yourself concentrating more on taking notes rather than on learning what was being presented?

Figure 3.6 shows what happens when we shorten the learning time to 20 minutes. The down-time is about 2 minutes or 10 percent of the total lesson time. As we shorten the learning episode, the down-time decreases faster than the prime-times. This research indicates that there is a higher probability of effective learning taking place if we can keep the learning episodes short and, of course, meaningful. Thus, teaching two 20-minute lessons provides 20 percent more prime-time (approximately 36 minutes) than one 40-minute lesson (approximately 30 minutes). Note, however, that a time period shorter than 20 minutes usually does not give the learner's brain sufficient time to determine the pattern and organization of the new learning, and is thus of little benefit.

The table above summarizes the approximate number of minutes in the prime-times and down-times of the learning cycle for episodes of 20, 40, and 80 minutes.

Figure 3.7 shows the gain in prime time that results from teaching two 20-minute lessons over one 40-minute lesson. Remember that the times are averages over many episodes. Nonetheless, these data confirm what we may have suspected: More retention occurs when lessons are shorter.

Retention Varies with Teaching Method

The learner's ability to retain information is also dependent on the type of teaching method used. Some methods result in more retention of learning than others. The learning pyramid in Figure 3.8, devised by the National Training Laboratories of Bethel, Maine, comes from studies on retention of learning after students were exposed to

Lecture continues to be the most prevalent teaching mode in secondary and higher education, despite overwhelming evidence that it produces the lowest degree of retention for most learners.

different teaching methods. The pyramid shows the percentage of new learning that students can recall after 24 hours as a result of being taught *primarily* by the teaching method indicated. The percentages are not additive. At the top of the pyramid is lecture—the teaching method that results in an average retention of only 5 percent of learn-

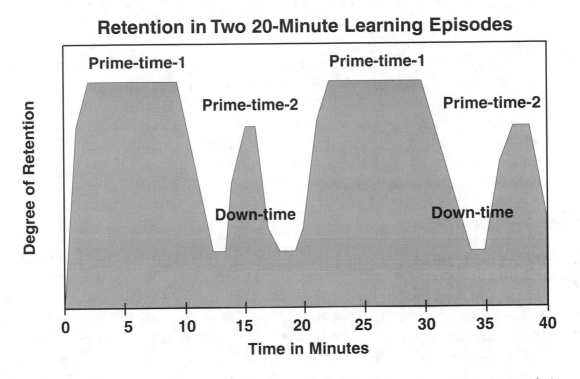

Figure 3.7. The graph illustrates how two 20-minute lessons are likely to result in more prime-time retention than one 40-minute lesson.

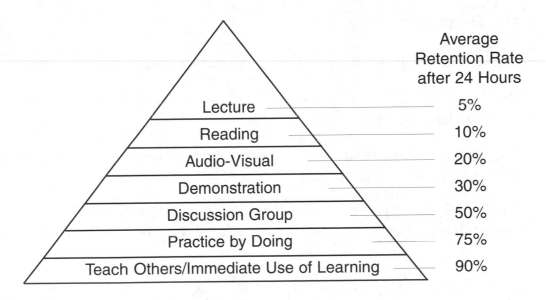

Figure 3.8. The learning pyramid shows the average percentage of retention of material after 24 hours for each of these instructional methods.

ing after 24 hours. This result is not surprising since lecture usually involves little student active participation or mental rehearsal. In this format, the teacher is telling and the students are listening just enough to convert the teacher's auditory and visual input into written notes. Rote rehearsal predominates and elaborative rehearsal is minimal or nonexistent. Despite the impressive amount of evidence about how little students retain from lecture, it continues to be the most prevalent mode of teaching, especially in secondary and higher education.

Moving down the pyramid, students become more involved in the learning process, and retention increases. The method at the bottom of the pyramid involves having the students teach others or use the new learning immediately. This results in over 90 percent retention after 24 hours. We have known for a long time that the best way to learn something is to prepare to teach it. In other words, whoever explains, learns. This is one of the major components of cooperative learning groups and helps to explain the effectiveness of this instructional technique.

Retention Through Practice

Practice refers to learners repeating a skill over time. It begins with the rehearsal of the new learning in working memory. Later, the memory is recalled from long-term storage and additional rehearsal follows. The quality of the rehearsals and the learner's knowledge base will largely determine the outcome of each practice.

The old adage that "practice makes perfect" is rarely true. It is very possible to practice the same skill repeatedly with no increase in achievement or accuracy of application. Think of the people you know who have been driving, cooking, or even teaching for many years with no improvement in their skills. Why is this? How is it possible for one to continuously practice a skill with no resulting improvement in performance?

Conditions for Successful Practice

For practice to *improve* performance, three conditions must be met (Hunter, 1982):

1. The learner must have all the knowledge necessary to understand the options available in applying the new knowledge or skill.

2. The learner must understand the steps in the process of applying the knowledge to deal with a particular situation.

3. The learner must be able to analyze the results of that application and know what variables need to be manipulated to improve performance in the future.

Teachers help learners meet these conditions when they:

- Start by selecting the smallest amount of material that will have maximum meaning for the learner.

- Model the application process step by step.

- Insist that the practice occur in their presence over a short period of time while the student is focused on the learning.

- Watch the practice and provide the students with prompt and specific feedback on what variable needs to be altered to correct and enhance the performance.

This strategy leads to perfect practice, and "Perfect practice makes perfect."

Practice and Feedback

Practice does make permanent, thereby aiding in the retention of learning. Consequently, we want to ensure that students practice the new learning correctly from the beginning. This early practice (referred to as *guided practice*), then, is done in the presence of the teacher who can now offer corrective feedback to help students analyze and improve their practice. When the practice is correct, the teacher can then assign *independent practice*, in which the students can rehearse the skill on their own to enhance retention.

Teachers should avoid giving students independent practice before guided practice. Since practice makes permanent, allowing students to rehearse something for the first time while away from the teacher is very risky. If they unknowingly practice the skill incorrectly, then they will learn the incorrect method well! This will present serious problems for both the teacher and learner later on because it is very difficult to change a skill that has been practiced and remembered, even if it is not correct.

Practice Over Time

Hunter (1982) suggested that teachers use two different types of practice over time, massed and distributed. Practicing a new learning during time periods that are very close together is called *massed practice*. This produces fast learning, as when you may mentally rehearse a new telephone number if you are unable to write it down.

Teachers provide massed practice when they allow students to try different examples of applying new learning in a short period of time. Cramming for an exam is an example of massed practice. Material can be quickly chunked into working memory, but can also be quickly dropped or forgotten if more sustained practice does not follow soon. This happens because the material has no further meaning and the need for long-term retention disappears.

> **Practice does not make perfect. Practice makes permanent. However, perfect practice makes perfect!**

Sustained practice over time, called *distributed practice*, is the key to retention. If you want to remember that new telephone number later on, you will need to use it repeatedly over time. Thus, practice that is dis-

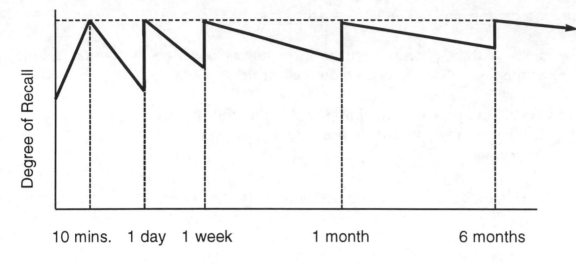

Figure 3.9. Practice over time (distributed practice) increases the degree of recall of learnings.

tributed over longer periods of time sustains meaning and consolidates the learnings into long-term storage in a form that will ensure accurate recall and applications in the future. The graph in Figure 3.9 shows that recall after periodic review improves over time. This is the reason behind the idea of the spiral curriculum whereby critical information and skills are reviewed at regular intervals within and over several grade levels.

Effective practice, then, starts with massed practice for fast learning and proceeds to distributed practice later for retention. This means that the student is continually practicing previously learned skills throughout the year. Each test should not only test new material, but should also allow students to practice older learnings. This method not only helps in retention, but reminds students that the learnings will be useful for the future and not just for the time when they were first learned.

Intelligence and Retrieval

Intelligence

Multiple Intelligences. Our modern notion of what constitutes human intelligence is growing increasingly complex. At the very least, it represents a combination of varied abilities and skills. The work of researchers such as Howard Gardner and Robert Sternberg has changed our view of intelligence from a singular entity to a multi-faceted aptitude that varies even within the same person. Gardner (1983) is convinced that at least seven different intelligences exist for each individual.[9] This theory suggests that at the core of each intelligence is an information-processing system (similar perhaps to that in

9. Gardner's seven intelligences are: musical, logical-mathematical, spatial, bodily-kinesthetic, linguistic, interpersonal, and intrapersonal.

Chapter 2) unique to that intelligence. The intelligence of an athlete is different from that of a musician or physicist. He also suggests that each intelligence is semi-autonomous. A person who has abilities in athletics but who does poorly in music has enhanced athletic intelligence. The presence or absence of music capabilities exists separately from the individual's athletic prowess.

Working Definition of Intelligence

We need a working definition of intelligence that reflects modern theory and is useful for practitioners. I offer this one: Intelligence is the *rate of learning* something. Although we are defining this complex concept with only three words, we need to understand them thoroughly. "Rate" is the amount of learning per unit of time. "Learning" is acquiring the information or skill through the application level of Bloom's Taxonomy (Chapter 6), so that it can be used to solve problems. Thus, "rate of learning" means the number of units of time one needs to acquire information or a skill at a level that can be used to solve problems correctly. By applying Gardner's concept of multiple intelligences, an individual can acquire different types of learning at different rates. One could learn to play several musical instruments quickly and competently, but have difficulty learning mathematics.

> **Our modern view of intelligence sees it as a multifaceted aptitude that varies even within the same individual. It can be defined as the rate of learning something.**

Using the rate of learning as the major criterion implies that intelligence is primarily a matter of neural efficiency. Could it be that intelligence describes the speed of the process whereby the brain eventually learns to use fewer neurons or networks to accomplish a repetitive task? If so, think of the implications this concept has for altering the way we allocate learning time, and design and deliver lessons. It suggests, at the very least, that we should vary learning time to accommodate the task at hand, and move learners to intensive practice as soon as comprehension is established.

Retrieval

It takes less than 50 milliseconds (a millisecond is 1/1000th of a second) to retrieve an item from working memory. Retrieving a memory from long-term storage, however, can be complicated and comparatively time-consuming. The brain uses two methods to retrieve information from long-term storage.

Recognition. Recognition matches an outside stimulus with stored information. For example, the questions on a multiple-choice test involve recognizing the correct answer (assuming the learner stored it originally) among the choices. This method helps explain why even poor students almost always do better than expected on multiple-choice tests.

Recall. Recall is quite different and more difficult. It describes the process whereby cues or hints are sent to long-term memory, which must search and retrieve information from long-term storage, then consolidate and decode it back into working memory.

Both methods require the firing of neurons along the neural pathways to the storage site(s) and back again to working memory. The more frequently we access a pathway, the less likely it is to be obscured by other pathways. Information we use frequently, such as our name and telephone number, are quickly retrieved because the neural impulses to and from those storage sites keep the pathways clear. When the information is moved into working memory, we reprocess it to determine its validity and, in effect, relearn it.

The rate at which the retrieval occurs depends on a number of factors, one of which is the system the student used to store the information originally. Students store the same item of information in different net-

> **Every time we retrieve something from long-term storage into working memory we relearn it.**

works, depending on how they link the information to their past learnings. These storage decisions affect the amount of time it will take these students to retrieve the information later. This explains why some students need more time than others to retrieve the same information. When teachers call on the first hands that go up, they inadvertently signal to the slower retrievers to stop the retrieval process. This is an unfortunate strategy for two reasons: First, the slower retrieving students feel that they are not getting teacher recognition, thereby lowering their self-concept. Second, by not retrieving the information into working memory, they miss an opportunity to relearn it.

Rates of Learning and Retrieval. In the information processing model in Chapter 2, the rate of learning (our working definition of intelligence) is represented by the data arrows flowing from left to right (from the senses through the perceptual register) to short-term memory and into working memory. The rate of retrieval is represented by the re-call arrow moving information from right to

> **Calling on the first hands that go up signals slower retrievers to stop the retrieval process.**

left, i.e., from long-term storage to working memory. *These two rates are independent of each other.* This notion is quite different from classic doctrine that holds that the retrieval rate is strongly related to intelligence, and thus anchored in genetic inheritance. The doctrine is further fueled in our society by timed tests and quiz programs that use the speed of retrieving answers as the main criterion for judging success and intelligence. The disclosure that the rate of retrieval is linked to the nature of the learner's storage method—a learned skill—rather than to intelligence is indeed significant. Since it is a *learned* skill, it can be taught. There is now great promise that techniques can be developed for helping us refine our storage methods for faster and more accurate retrieval. Some of those techniques are in the **Practitioner's Corners** at the end of this chapter.

Since the rate of learning and the rate of retrieval are independent, individuals can be fast or slow learners, fast or slow retrievers, and every combination in between. While most people tend to fall mid-range, some are at the extremes. Actually, not only have we had experience with learners possessing the extreme combinations of these two rates, but we have (unwittingly) made up

> **The rate of learning and the rate of retrieval are independent of each other.**

> **Test Question No. 5:** *The rate at which a learner retrieves information from memory is closely related to intelligence.*
>
> **Answer:** *False. The rate of retrieval is independent of intelligence. It is more closely tied to how and where the information was stored originally.*

labels to describe them. An individual who is a fast learner and a fast retriever we call a *genius*. These students retrieve answers quickly. Their hands go up first. Their responses are almost always correct, and they get reputations as "brains." Teachers call on them when they want to keep the lesson moving.

A fast learner and slow retriever we call an *underachiever*. Teachers usually say to these students, "Come on, John, I know you know this … keep trying." We often run out of patience and admonish them for not studying enough. A slow learner and fast retriever, we call an *overachiever*. These students may respond quickly, but their answers may be incorrect. Teachers sometimes mistakenly view them as trying too hard to learn something that may be beyond them.

For a slow learner and slow retriever, we have a whole list of uncomplimentary labels. More regrettable is that too often we interpret "slow learner" to mean "unable to learn." What being a slow learner really means is that the student is unable to learn something in the amount of time we have arbitrarily assigned for that learning. All

> **Too often we interpret slow learner to mean unable to learn.**

these labels are unfortunate since they perpetuate the mistaken notion that the major factors promoting successful learning are beyond the control of the learner and teacher.

Chunking

Is it possible to consciously increase the number of items that working memory can handle at one time? The answer is yes, through a process called *chunking*. Chunking occurs when working memory perceives a set of data as a single item, much as we perceive *information* as one word (and, therefore, one item) even though it is composed of 11 separate letters. Going back to the number exercise in Chapter 2, some people may have indeed remembered all 10 digits in the right sequence. These may be people who spend a lot of time on the telephone. When they see a 10-digit number, their experience helps them to group it by area code, prefix, and extension. Thus, they see the second number, 4915082637, as (491) 508–2637, which is in 3 chunks, not 10. Since 3 are within the working memory's functional capacity, they can remember it accurately.

Effect of Experience

Let's take this a step further. Look at the following sentence:

Test Question No. 6: *The amount of information a learner can deal with at one time is genetically linked.*

Answer: *False. The amount of information a learner can deal with at one time is linked to the learner's ability to add more items to the chunks in working memory—a learned skill.*

Grandma is buying an apple.

This sentence has 22 letters, but only five chunks (or words) of information. Since the sentence is one complete thought, most people treat it as just one item in working memory. In this example, 22 bits of data (letters) become one chunk (complete thought). Visual learners probably formed a mental image of a grandmother buying that apple.

Now let's add more information to working memory. Stare at the next sentence below for about 10 seconds. Now close your eyes and try recalling the two sentences.

Hte plpae si edr.

Having trouble with the second? That's because the words make no sense and working memory is treating each of the 13 letters and three spaces as 16 individual items (plus the first sentence as 1 item, for a total of 17). The 5–9 item functional capacity range of working memory is quickly exceeded.

Let's rearrange the letters in each word of the second sentence to read as follows:

The apple is red.

Stare at this sentence for 10 seconds. Now close your eyes again and try to remember the first sentence and this sentence. Most people will remember both sentences since they are now just 2 items instead of 17, and their meanings are related. Experience, once again, helps the working memory decide how to chunk items.

Here's a frequently-used example of how experience can help in chunking information and improving achievement. Get the pencil and paper again. Now stare at the letters below for 10 seconds. Then look away from the page and write them down in the correct sequence and groupings. Ready? Go.

LSDN BCT VF BIU SA

Check your results. Did you get all the letters in the correct sequence and groupings? Probably not, but that's OK. Most people would not get 100 percent by staring at the letters in such a short period of time.

Let's try it again. Same rules: Stare at the letters below for 10 seconds and write the letters down. Ready? Go.

LSD NBC TV FBI USA

How did you do this time? Most people do much better on this example. Now compare the two examples. Note that the letters in both examples are *identical and in the same sequence!* The only difference is that the letters in the second example are grouped or chunked in a way that allows experience to help working memory process and hold the items. Working memory saw the first example as 14 letters plus four spaces (since the grouping was important) or 18 items—much more than its functional capacity. But the second example was quickly seen as only 5 understandable items (the spaces no longer mattered) and thus within the limits of its capacity. Some people may have even paired NBC with TV, and FBI with USA, so that they actually dealt with just three chunks. These examples show the power of experience in remembering—a principle of learning called *transfer,* which we will discuss in the next chapter.

Chunking is a very effective way of enlarging working memory's capacity. It can be used to memorize a long string of numbers or words. Most of us learned the alphabet in chunks—for some it may have been abcd, efg, hijk, lmnop, qrs, tuv, wxyz. Chunking reduced the 26 letters to a smaller number of items that working memory could handle. Even people can be chunked, such as couples (e.g., Romeo and Juliet, Abbott and Costello, Bonnie and Clyde), in which recalling the name of one immediately suggests the name of the other. Master chess players remember the chess board by chunking the individual pieces into meaningful clusters. This reduces the board to a few chunks and leaves room in working memory for additional information and processing. Although working memory has a functional capacity limit as to the number of chunks it can process at one time, there appears to be no limit to the number of items that can be combined into a chunk.

> **Chunking is an effective way of enlarging working memory's capacity and for helping the learner make associations that establish meaning.**

Cramming

Cramming for a test or interview is another example of chunking. The learner loads into working memory as many items as can be identified as needed. Varying degrees of temporary associations are made among the items. With sufficient effort and meaning, the items can be carried in working memory, even for hours, until needed. If the source of the crammed items was outside the learner, that is, from texts or class notes, then it is possible for none of the crammed items to be transferred to long-term storage. This practice (which many of us have experienced) explains how a learner can be conversant and outwardly competent in the items tested on one day (while the items were in working memory) and have little or no understanding of them several days later after they drop out of working memory into oblivion. We cannot recall what we have not stored. See the **Practitioner's Corner** on "Testing Whether Information is in Long-Term Storage" in Chapter 2.

Test Question No. 7: *It is usually not possible to increase the amount of information that the working memory can deal with at one time.*

Answer: *False. By increasing the number of items in a chunk, we can increase the amount of information that our working memory can process simultaneously.*

Forgetting

What happens to memories in long-term storage over time? The answer to this question has now changed because of new research. Until recently, we thought that the storage sites deteriorated naturally over time due to subtle changes in the structure and orientation of the molecules at the dendrite spines located in the memory site synapses. As these changes continued, more of the memory would be distorted or lost, resulting in *forgetting*. Recent studies of brain-damaged patients (Rose, 1992) suggest, however, that forgetting is not due to the deterioration of the memory sites, but more likely to *losing the pathways* to the sites. Apparently, this happens when we do not recall a memory for a long time. The pathway to older learning is obscured by new pathways formed to more recent memories that now interfere with recalling the older memory. The older memory, however, seems to remain unchanged throughout the life of the individual.

Does it make a difference whether forgetting is the deterioration of the memory sites or losing the pathways? Is not the result the same, the inability to recall the memory? Sure, the result *is* the same, but since our understanding of the storage process has changed, so has the method for trying to recall it. We can use a therapy that helps us to find the original pathway, or an alternate pathway, to the memory sites.

Here is an example. Suppose you try to recall the name of the teacher you had when you were in second grade. Unless you have thought recently about that teacher, the pathway to that name has not been used for a long time. It is blocked by newer pathways, and you will have difficulty finding it. The name is still there, but it may take you as long as several days to find it. It will probably come to you when you least expect it.

Another example: Suppose you start thinking about finding an old sweater that you have not seen in several years. If you believe you gave it away, you will not even begin to look for it. That is the same as if you believe that your forgotten memory has been destroyed over time; you will not even try to recall it. On the other hand, if you are con-

Test Question No. 8: *Recent research confirms that information in long-term storage deteriorates as we get older.*

Answer: *False. Pathways to older memory sites get obstructed by newer pathways.*

vinced that the sweater is somewhere in that big attic, then it is just a matter of time before your hunt pays off and you find it. You'll probably start by thinking of the last time you wore it.

This is the same process memory therapy uses with brain-damaged individuals. The therapy helps the patient seek other neural connections to find the original or an alternate pathway to the memory sites. We'll discuss this storage process more in Chapter 4 when we look at the transfer of learnings.

Confabulation

Have you ever been discussing an experience with someone who had shared it with you and started arguing over some of the details? As described earlier, long-term memory is the process of searching, locating, retrieving, and transferring information to working memory. Rote recall, especially of frequently used information, such as your name and address, is actually simple. These pathways are clear and retrieval time is very short. Retrieving more complex and less-frequently used concepts is much more complicated. It requires signaling multiple storage sites through elaborate, cluttered pathways for intermediate consolidation and ultimate decoding into working memory. It is less accurate. First, most do not retain 100 percent of elaborate experiences, such as an extensive vacation. Second, we store parts of the experience in many storage areas.

When retrieving such an experience, the long-term memory may not be able to locate all the events being requested, either because of insufficient time or because they were never retained. In this case, it unconsciously fabricates the missing or incomplete information by selecting the next closest item it can recall. This process is called *confabulation* and occurs because the brain is always active and creative, and seems to abhor incompleteness. It is *not* lying, since confabulation is an unconscious rather than a deliberate process, and the individual believes the fabricated information to be true. This explains why two people who participated in the same experience will recall slightly—or even significantly—different versions of the same event. Neither individual stored 100 percent of the experience. If they stored 90 percent, it would not be the *same* 90 percent for both. Their missing and different 10 percents will be fabricated and will cause each to question the accuracy of the other's memory. The less of the experience remembered, the more the brain must fabricate.

> **Our brain fabricates information and experiences that we believe to be true.**

Over time, the fabricated parts are consolidated into the memory network. As we systematically recall this memory, minor alterations may continue to be made through confabulation. Gradually the original memory is transformed and encoded into a considerably different one that we believe to be true and accurate.

This also happens in the classroom. When recalling a complex learning, the learner is unaware of which parts were missing and, thus, fabricated. The younger the learner, the more inconsistent the fabricated parts are likely to be. The teacher may react by thinking the student is inventing answers intentionally and may discipline accordingly.

Rather, the teacher should be aware of confabulation as a possibility, identify the fabricated parts, and provide the feedback needed to help the student correct the inaccurate material. Through practice, the learner will then incorporate the corrected material into memory and transfer it to long-term storage.

Confabulation has implications for the justice system. This tendency for the brain to fabricate information rather than admit its absence can have serious consequences in court trials where eyewitnesses, under the pressure of testifying, feel compelled to provide complete information. Confabulation also raises questions about the accuracy of witnesses recalling very old memories of unpleasant events, such as a childhood accident or abuse. Experiments done by Loftus (1995) have shown how easy it is to distort a person's recollection of even recent events, or to "implant" memories. In the absense of independent verification, it is impossible to decide what events in the recalled "repressed memory" actually occurred and which are the result of confabulation.

PRACTITIONER'S CORNER

Using Rehearsal To Enhance Retention

Rehearsal refers to the learner's reprocessing of new information in an attempt to determine sense and meaning. It occurs in two forms. Some information items have value only if they are remembered *exactly* as presented, such as the letters and sequence of the alphabet, spelling, poetry, telephone numbers, and the multiplication tables. This is called *rote rehearsal.* Sense and meaning are established quickly and the likelihood of long-term retention is high. Most of us can recall poems and telephone numbers that we learned many years ago.

More complex concepts require the learner to make connections and to form associations and other relationships in order to establish sense and meaning. Thus, the information may need to be reprocessed several times as new links are found. This is called *elaborative rehearsal.* The more senses that are used in this elaborative rehearsal, the more reliable the associations. Thus, when visual, auditory, and kinesthetic activities assist the learner during this rehearsal, the probability of long-term storage rises dramatically. That is why it is important for students to talk about what they are learning *while* they are learning it, and to have visual models as well.

Rehearsal is teacher-initiated and teacher-directed. Recognizing that rehearsal is a necessary ingredient for retention of learning, teachers should consider the following when designing and presenting their lessons:

Rote Rehearsal Strategies

- **Simple Repetition.** For remembering short items (telephone numbers, names, and dates) this is simply repeating a set of items over and over until they can be recalled in correct sequence.

- **Cumulative Repetition.** For longer sets of items (song, poem, list of battles) the learner rehearses the first few items. Then the next set of items in the sequence is added to the first set for the next rehearsal, and so on. To remember a poem of four stanzas, the learner rehearses the first stanza, then rehearses the second stanza alone, then the two together, then rehearses the third stanza, then the three stanzas together, etc.

PRACTITIONER'S CORNER

Using Rehearsal To Enhance Retention – Continued

Elaborative Rehearsal Strategies

- **Paraphrasing.** Students orally restate ideas in their own words, which then become familiar cues for later storage. Using auditory modality helps the learner attach sense, making retention more likely.

- **Selecting and Notetaking.** Students review texts, illustrations, and lectures and decide which portions are critical and important. They make these decisions based on criteria from the teacher, authors, or other students. The students then paraphrase the idea and write it into their notes. Adding the kinesthetic exercise of writing furthers retention.

- **Predicting.** After studying a section of content, the students predict the material to follow or what questions the teacher might ask about that content. Prediction keeps students focused on the new content, adds interest, and helps them apply prior learnings to new situations, thus aiding retention.

- **Questioning.** After studying content, students generate questions about the content. To be effective, the questions should range from lower-level thinking of recall, comprehension, and application to higher-level thinking of analysis, synthesis, and evaluation (see Bloom's Taxonomy in Chapter 6). When designing questions of varying complexity, students engage in deeper cognitive processing, clarify concepts, and predict meaning and associations—all contributors to retention.

- **Summarizing.** Students reflect on and summarize in their heads the important material or skills learned in the lesson. This is often the last and critical stage where students can attach sense and meaning to the new learning. Summarizing rehearsal is also called closure (see the **Practitioner's Corner** on *closure* on p. 28 for further explanation).

Note on Constructivism. Those familiar with constructivism will recognize that the above strategies are consistent with the practices associated with that theory of learning.

PRACTITIONER'S CORNER

Using Rehearsal To Enhance Retention – Continued
General Guidelines

If the retention of new information or skill beyond the immediate lesson is an important expectation, then rehearsal must be a crucial part of the learner's processing. The considerations below should be incorporated into decisions about using rehearsal.

- **Teach** students rehearsal activities and strategies. As soon as they recognize the differences between rote and elaborative rehearsal, they can understand the importance of selecting the appropriate type for each learning objective. With practice, they should quickly realize that fact and data acquisition require rote rehearsal, while analysis and evaluation of concepts require elaborative rehearsal.

- **Remind** students to continuously practice rehearsal strategies until they become regular parts of their study and learning habits.

- **Keep** rehearsal relevant. Effective elaborative rehearsal relies more on making personally meaningful associations to prior learning than on time-consuming efforts that lack these student-centered connections. Associations that center in the teacher's experiences may not be relevant to students.

- **Remember** that time alone is not a trustworthy indicator of the extent of rehearsal. The degree of meaning associated with the new learning is much more significant than the time allotted.

- **Have** learners verbalize their rehearsal to peers or teachers while they are learning new material as this increases the likelihood of retention.

- **Provide** more visual and contextual clues to make rehearsal meaningful and successful for some students. Those with limited verbal competence will focus on visual and concrete lesson components to assist in their rehearsal. This will be particularly true of students whose native language is not English.

PRACTITIONER'S CORNER

Using the Primacy-Recency Effect in the Classroom

The primacy-recency effect describes the phenomenon whereby, during a learning episode, we tend to remember best that which comes first (prime-time-1), we remember second best that which comes last (prime-time-2), and we remember least that which comes just past the middle (down-time). This effect can lead to lessons that are more likely to be remembered when the teacher considers the following:

- **Teach the new material first** (after getting the students' focus) during prime-time-1. This is the time of greatest retention.

- **Avoid** asking students at the beginning of the lesson if they know anything about the topic being introduced. Since this is the time of greatest retention, almost anything that is said, including *incorrect* information, is likely to be remembered. Give the information and examples yourself to ensure they are correct.

- **Avoid** using precious prime-time periods for classroom management tasks, such as collecting absence notes or taking attendance. Do these before you get focus or during the down-time.

- **Use the down-time** portion to have students practice the new learning or to discuss it by relating it to past learnings.

- **Do closure** during prime-time-2. This is the learner's last opportunity to attach sense and meaning to the new learning, to make decisions about it, and to determine where and how it will be transferred to long-term storage.

- **Try to package lesson objectives** (or sub-learnings) in teaching episodes of about 20 minutes. Link the sublearnings according to the total time period available, e.g., two 20-minute lessons for a 40-minute teaching period, three for an hour period, and so on.

PRACTITIONER'S CORNER

Using Practice Effectively

Practice does not make perfect. It makes *permanent*. The purpose of practice is to allow the learner to use the newly-learned skill in a new situation with sufficient accuracy so that it will be correctly remembered and stored. Before allowing the students to begin practice, the teacher should model the thinking process involved and guide the class through each step of the new learning's application. Since practice makes permanent, the teacher should monitor the students' early practice to ensure that it is accurate and to provide timely feedback and correction if it is not. This guided practice helps eliminate initial errors and alerts the students to the critical steps in applying the new skill. Here are some considerations suggested by Hunter (1982) when guiding initial practice:

- **Amount of Material To Practice.** Practice should be limited to the smallest amount of material or skill that has the most meaning for the students. This allows for sense and meaning to be consolidated as the learner uses the new learning.

- **Amount of Time To Practice.** Practice should take place in short, intense periods of time when the student's working memory is running on prime time. When the practice period is short, students are more likely to be intent on learning what they are practicing.

- **Frequency of Practice.** New learning should be practiced frequently at first so that it is quickly consolidated into long-term storage. This is called *massed practice.* If we expect students to retain the information in active storage and to remember how to use it accurately, it should continue to be practiced over longer time intervals. This is called *distributed practice* and is the real key to accurate retention and application of information and skills over time.

- **Accuracy of Practice.** As students move through guided practice, it is important for the teacher to give prompt and specific feedback as to whether the practice is correct or incorrect and why. This process also gives the teacher valuable information about the degree of student understanding and whether it makes sense to move on or reteach portions that may be difficult for some students.

PRACTITIONER'S CORNER

Relearning Through Recall

Every time we recall information from long-term storage into working memory, we relearn it. Therefore, teachers should use classroom strategies that encourage students to recall previously-learned information regularly so they will relearn it. One strategy for doing this is to maintain learner participation throughout the lesson. Hunter (1982) calls this *active participation*. This principle of learning attempts to keep the mind of the student consistently focused on what is being learned or recalled through covert and overt activities.

The covert activity involves the teacher asking the students to recall previously learned information and to process it in some way. It could be, "Think of the conditions that existed in America just after the Civil War that we learned yesterday, and be prepared to discuss them in a few minutes." This statement informs the students that they will be held accountable for their recall. This accountability increases the likelihood that the students will recall the desired item and, thus, relearn it. It also alleviates the need for the teacher to call on every student to determine if the recall occurred. After sufficient wait time (see the **Practitioner's Corner** on the next page), overt activities are used to determine the quality of the covert recall.

Some suggestions on how to use active participation strategies effectively:

- **State the question** and allow thinking time *before* calling on a student for response. This holds all students accountable for recalling the answer until you pick your first respondent.

- **Give clear and specific directions** as to what the students should recall. Focus on the lesson objectives and not on the activities unless they were a crucial part of the learning. Repeat the question using different words and phraseology. This increases the number of cues that the learners have during their retrieval search.

- **Avoid predictable patterns** when calling on students, such as alphabetical order, up and down rows, or raised hands. These patterns signal the students *when* they will be held accountable, thereby allowing them to go off task before and after their turns.

PRACTITIONER'S CORNER

Using Wait Time To Increase Student Participation

Wait time refers to the period of teacher silence that follows the posing of a question before the first student is called on for a response. Regrettably, studies such as those conducted by Mary Budd Rowe (1974, 1978) of the University of Florida in Gainesville indicate that high school teachers had an average wait time of just over one second. Elementary teachers waited an average of three seconds. This was hardly enough time for slower retrievers, many of whom may know the correct answer, to locate that answer in long-term storage and retrieve it into working memory. Remember that as soon as the teacher calls on the first student, the remaining students **stop the retrieval process** and lose the opportunity to **re-learn** the information.

Rowe found that when teachers extended the wait time to at least **five** seconds or more:

- The length and quality of student responses increased

- There was greater participation by slower learners

- Students used more evidence to support inferences

- There were more higher-order responses.

These results occurred at all grade levels and in all subjects.

Rowe also noted positive changes in the behavior of teachers who consistently used wait time. Specifically, she observed these teachers:

- Used more higher-order questioning

- Demonstrated greater flexibility in evaluating responses

- Improved their expectations for the performance of slower learners.

There are many ways that teachers can use wait time in their classes. One effective method is called Think-Pair-Share, and is frequently used in cooperative learning groups. In this strategy, the teacher asks the students to think about a question. After adequate wait time, the students form pairs and exchange the results of their thinking. This is followed by asking some students to share their ideas with the entire class.

PRACTITIONER'S CORNER

Using Chunking To Enhance Retention

Chunking is the process whereby the brain perceives several items of information as a single item. Words are common examples of chunks. *Elephant* is composed of eight letters, but the brain perceives them as one item of information. The more items we can put into a chunk, the more information we can process in working memory and remember at one time. Chunking is a learned skill and, thus, can also be taught.

Pattern Chunking: This is most easily accomplished whenever we can find patterns in the material to be retained.

- Say we wanted to remember the number 3421941621776. Without a pattern, these 13 digits are treated as separate items and exceed working memory's functional capacity of about seven items. But we could arrange the numbers in groups that have meaning. For example, 342 (my house number), 1941 (when World War II began), 62 (my father's age), and 1776 (the Declaration of Independence). Now the number is only four chunks with meaning: 342 1941 62 1776.

- This example, admittedly contrived, shows how chunking can work at different levels. The task is to memorize the following string of words:

  COW GRASS FIELD TENNIS NET SODA DOG LAKE FISH

  We need a method to remember the sequence, since nine is more than the functional capacity of seven. We can chunk the sequence of items by using a simple story. First we see a **cow** eating **grass** in a **field**. Also in the field are two people playing **tennis**. One player hits the ball way over the **net**. They are drinking **soda** while their **dog** runs after the ball that went into the **lake**. The dog's splashing frightens the **fish**.

- Learning a step-by-step procedure for tying a shoelace or copying a computer file from a floppy to a hard disk are examples of pattern chunking. We group the items in a sequence and rehearse it mentally until it becomes one or a few chunks. Practicing the procedure further enhances the formation of chunks.

These examples show how information can be chunked in patterns. Learners can be shown other patterns and should select those that work best for them.

PRACTITIONER'S CORNER

Using Chunking To Enhance Retention – Continued

Categorical Chunking: This is a more sophisticated chunking process in that the learner establishes various types of categories to help classify large amounts of information. The learner reviews the information looking for criteria that will group complex material into simpler categories or arrays. The different types of categories can include:

- **Advantages and Disadvantages**. The information is categorized according to the pros and cons of the concept. Examples include energy use, abortion, and capital punishment.

- **Similarities and Differences**. The learner compares two or more concepts using attributes that make them similar and different. Examples are comparing the Articles of Confederation to the Bill of Rights, mitosis to meiosis, and the U.S. Civil War to the Vietnam War.

- **Structure and Function**. These categories are helpful with concepts that have parts with different functions, such as identifying the parts of an animal cell, a carburetor, or the human digestive system.

- **Taxonomies**. This system sorts information into hierarchical levels according to certain common characteristics. Examples are biological taxonomies (kingdom, phylum, class, etc.), taxonomies of learning (cognitive, affective, and psychomotor), and governmental bureaucracies.

- **Arrays**. These are less ordered than taxonomies in that the criteria for establishing the array are not always logical, but are more likely based on observable features. Human beings are classified, for example, by learning style and personality type. Dogs can be grouped by size, shape, or fur length. Clothing can be divided by material, season, and gender.

Making categorical chunking a regular part of classroom instruction can raise student learning, thinking, and retention significantly.

PRACTITIONER'S CORNER

Using Mnemonics To Help Retention

Mnemonics (from the Greek "to remember") are very useful devices for re-membering unrelated information, patterns, or rules. They were developed by the ancient Greeks to help them remember dialogue in plays and for passing information to others when writing was impractical. There are many types of mnemonic schemes. Here are two that can be easily used in the classroom. Work with students to develop schemes appropriate for the content.

- **Rhyming Mnemonics**. Rhymes are simple and effective ways to remember rules and patterns. They work because if you forget part of the rhyme or get part of it wrong, the words lose their rhyme or rhythm and signal the error. To retrieve the missing or incorrect part you start the rhyme over again, and this helps you to relearn it. Have you ever tried to remember the fifth line of a song or poem without starting at the beginning? It is very difficult to do since each line serves as the auditory cue for the next line.

  Common examples of rhymes we have learned are "*I* before *e*, except after *c* ...," "Thirty days hath September ...," and "Columbus sailed the ocean blue ... "

  Here are rhymes that can help students learn information in other areas:

  > **The Spanish Armada met its fate**
  > **In fifteen hundred and eighty-eight.**
  >
  > **Divorced, beheaded, died;**
  > **Divorced, beheaded, survived.**
  > (The fate of Henry VIII's six wives, in chronological order.)
  >
  > **The number you are dividing by,**
  > **Turn upside down and multiply.**
  > (Rule for dividing by fractions.)

  This may seem like a clumsy system, but it works. Make up your own rhyme, alone or with the class, to help you and your students remember information.

PRACTITIONER'S CORNER

Using Mnemonics To Help Retention – Continued

- **Reduction Mnemonics**: In this scheme, you reduce a large body of information to a shorter form and use a letter to represent each shortened piece. The letters are either combined to form a real or artificial word or are used to construct a simple sentence. For example, the real word **HOMES** can help us remember the names of the great lakes (Huron, Ontario, Michigan, Erie, and Superior). The name **ROY G BIV** aids in remembering the seven colors of the spectrum (red, orange, yellow, green, blue, indigo, and violet). The artificial word **NATO** recalls North Atlantic Treaty Organization. The sentence **My Very Earnest Mother Just Served Us Nine Pizzas** can help us remember the nine planets of the solar system in order from the sun (Mercury, Venus, Earth, Mars, Jupiter, Uranus, Neptune, and Pluto). Here are other examples:

Please Excuse My Dear Aunt Sally
(The order for solving algebraic equations: Parenthesis, Exponents, Multiplication, Division, Addition, Subtraction.)

Frederick Charles Goes Down And Ends Battle
(F, C, G, D, A, E, B. The order that sharps are entered in key signatures; reverse the order for flats.)

McHALES
(The different forms of energy: Mechanical, Chemical, Heat, Atomic, Light, Electrical, and Solar.)

In Poland, Men Are Tall
(The stages of cell division in mitosis: Interphase, Prophase, Metaphase, Anaphase, and Telophase.)

Krakatoa Positively Casts Off Fumes, Generally Sulfurous Vapors
(The descending order of zoological classifications: Kingdom, Phylum, Class, Order, Family, Genus, Species, Variety.)

King Henry Doesn't Mind Drinking Cold Milk
(The descending order of metric prefixes: Kilo, Hecto, Deca, (measure), Deci, Centi, and Milli.)

CHAPTER *4*

THE POWER OF TRANSFER

*Transfer is the basis of all creativity, problem solving and
the making of satisfying decisions.*
— Madeline Hunter, *Mastery Teaching*

Chapter Highlights: This chapter explains the components of the most
powerful principle of learning, transfer. It examines the factors that affect transfer and how teachers can use past learnings effectively to enhance present and future learning.

The brain is a dynamic creation that is constantly organizing and reorganizing itself when it receives new stimuli. More networks are formed as raw items merge
into new patterns. Just as musicians in an orchestra join the individual sounds of
their instruments in new and melodious ways, so does the brain unite disconnected
ideas with wonderful harmony. We can add beauty and clarity, and forge isolated ideas
into spectacular visions. Transfer is one process that allows this amazing inventiveness
to unfold. It encompasses the ability to learn in one situation and then use that learning,
possibly in a modified or generalized form, in other situations. Transfer is the core of
problem solving, creative thinking, and all other higher mental processes, inventions,
and artistic products.

What Is Transfer?

The principle of learning called *transfer* describes a two-part process: (1) the effect that
past learning has on the processing of new learning, and (2) the degree to which the new
learning will be useful to the learner in the future (Hunter, 1982; Perkins and Salomon,
1988). The process goes something like this: Whenever new learning moves into working
memory, long-term memory (most likely stimulated by a signal from the hippocampus)
simultaneously searches the long-term storage sites for any past learnings that are simi-

lar to, or associated with, the new learning. If the experiences exist, they also move into working memory.

The degree to which past learning affects the learner's ability to acquire new knowledge or skills in another context describes one phase of the powerful phenomenon called transfer (Figure 4.1). In other words, the information processing system depends on past learnings to associate with, make sense of, and treat new information. This recycling of past information into the flow not only reinforces and provides additional rehearsal for already-stored information, but it aids in assigning meaning to new information. The degree of meaning attributed to new learning will determine the connections that are made between it and other information in long-term storage. These connections and associations give the learner more options to cope with new situations in the future.

Positive and Negative Transfer

Positive Transfer. When past learning helps the learner deal with new learning, it is called *positive transfer*. Suppose a violin player and a trombone player both want to learn to play the viola, an instrument similar to the violin. Who will learn the new instrument more easily? The violin player already possesses the skills and knowledge that will help in learning the viola. The trombone player, on the other hand, may be a very accomplished trombonist, but possesses few skills that will help to play the viola. Similarly, Michelangelo, DaVinci, and Edison were able to transfer a great deal of their knowledge and skills to create magnificent works of art and invention. Their prior learnings made greater achievement possible.

Figure 4.1. The effect that past learning has on the processing of new learning is part of transfer.

Negative Transfer. Sometimes past learning interferes with the learner's understanding of new learning, resulting in confusion or errors. This process is called *negative transfer*. If, for example, you have been driving cars only with automatic shift, you will have quite a surprise the first time you drive a standard shift car. You were accustomed to keeping your left foot idle or using it to brake. In either case, the left foot has a very different function in a standard-shift car. If it keeps doing its automatic-shift functions (or does nothing), you will have great difficulty driving the standard-shift car. In other words, the skills that the driver's brain assigned to the left foot for the automatic-shift car are not the skills it needs to cope with the standard-shift car. The skill it used before is interfering with the skill needed in the new situation, an example of negative transfer.

Transfer and Meaning

Meaning often results when past learning moves from long-term storage into working memory and interacts with new information. The diverse nature of an individual's experiences can impart different meanings to the same information. Consider the following pieces of information:

1. There are seven days in the week.
2. Force = mass x acceleration.
3. Iraq is an evil country.
4. ... they also serve who only stand and wait.
5. Jesus is the son of God.
6. There's a sucker born every minute.

In each instance, the meaning of the information depends on the experience, education, and state of mind of the reader. The third and last statements can arouse passionate agreement or disavowal. The second and fourth statements would be meaningless to a second grader, but not the first statement. The fifth could provoke an endless debate among adherents of different religions.

Meaning is often context dependent. The transfer process not only provides interpretation of words, but often includes nuances and shadings that can result in very different meanings. "He is a piece of work!" can be either a compliment or a sarcastic comment, depending on tone and context.

Transfer in the Curriculum

A review of any curriculum reveals that transfer is an integral component and expectation of the learning process. Every day, teachers deliberately or intuitively refer to past learning to make new learning more understandable and meaningful. For the long term, students are expected to transfer the knowledge and skills they learn in school to their daily routines, jobs, and ventures outside the school. Writing and speaking skills should help them communicate with others, scientific knowledge should inform their decisions on environmental and health issues, and their understanding of history should guide their responses to contemporary problems at personal, social, and cultural levels. It is almost axiomatic that the more information students can transfer from their schooling to the context of everyday life, the greater the probability that they will be good communicators, informed citizens, critical thinkers, and successful problem solvers.

Yet studies continue to show that students are not successful in recognizing how the skills and knowledge they learned in school apply to new situations they encounter outside school (Perkins and Salomon, 1988). Apparently, we are doing little in schools to deliberately make the transfer connections to enhance new learning. The more connections that students can make between past learning and new learning, the more likely they are to determine sense and meaning and thus retain the new learning. Moreover, when these connections can be extended across curriculum areas, they establish a framework of associative networks that will be recalled for future problem solving. Successful transfer can be enhanced by educators who advocate thematic units and an integrated curriculum. This approach helps students to see commonalities among diverse topics and to reinforce understanding and meaning for future applications.

> **Thematic units and an integrated curriculum enhance the transfer process.**

Transfer in the Classroom

During a lesson, students are dealing continually with transfer as they process and practice new information and skills. Since each student's experiences vary, the extent of what transfers also varies. Whether that transfer aids or impedes the acquisition of new learning is a major factor in determining the success each student has in accomplishing the lesson objective.

> **Teachers are frequently the provokers of transfer for their students.**

For example, teachers who teach Romance languages to native English-speakers are frequently helped by positive transfer and plagued by negative transfer. Words like *rouge* in French and *mucho* in Spanish help to teach *red* and *much*, respectively, but when students see the French *librairie* and are told it is a place where books are found, experience prompts them to think that it means *library*. It really means *bookstore*.

Transfer Provoked by Environment

Another interesting characteristic of transfer is that it is more frequently provoked by the environment than consciously by the learner. Have you ever heard a song that brings back a flood of memories? You could not really control that recall unless something else in your environment demanded your immediate attention, as your crying baby or a ringing fire alarm. Now, who represents a large portion of the environment for students in school? Yes, the teachers! Teachers are the instruments of transfer for students. If teachers are not aware of that, they can inadvertently provoke negative transfer during learning situations just as easily as they can provoke positive transfer. To use transfer effectively, teachers need to identify factors that facilitate learning (positive transfer) while minimizing or eliminating factors that can cause interference (negative transfer).

Test Question No. 9: *Most of the time, the transfer of information from long-term storage is under the conscious control of the learner.*

Answer: *False. The transfer process is more often provoked by the learner's environment.*

Example of Transfer in an English Class

The following anecdote illustrates how transfer can impede or promote a lesson objective. A few years ago, I observed a senior class in British Literature in a large urban high school. It was late April, and as the students entered the class they were discussing the upcoming final examinations, the prom, and preparations for graduation. After the opening bell rang, the teacher admonished the students to pay attention and said, "Today we are going to start another play by William Shakespeare." The moans and groans were deafening and abated only after the teacher used every threat short of ripping up their forthcoming diplomas. Judging from their reactions and unsolicited comments, the students' perceptions of their experiences with Shakespeare were hardly positive. Without realizing it, the teacher's meager introduction had provoked negative transfer; getting the students to focus constructively on the new play now would not be easy.

Later that afternoon, I found myself in a different teacher's British Literature class. A large television monitor and a videocassette recorder in the front of the classroom attracted the students as they entered. The teacher asked the students to watch a videotape and be prepared to discuss what they saw. What unfolded over the next 15 minutes was a cleverly edited collection of scenes from the movie *West Side Story*. There was enough to get the plot and enough of the music to maintain interest. The students were captivated; some even sang along. As the showdown between Tony and Maria's brother came on the screen, the teacher stopped the tape. The students complained, wanting to see who won the fight. The teacher noted that this was really an old story set in modern times, and that she had the script of the original play. The characters' names and the location were different, but the plot was the same. While the students were discussing what they had seen, she distributed Shakespeare's *Romeo and Juliet*. Many students eagerly flipped through the pages trying to find the outcome of the fight scene! The teacher's understanding of positive transfer was evident, and she used it magnificently.

Knowledge is power. Understanding how transfer helps or impedes learning gives teachers opportunities to use positive transfer and avoid negative transfer.

Factors Affecting Transfer

How quickly transfer occurs during a learning situation depends on the rate of retrieval. As noted earlier, the rate of retrieval is largely dependent on the storage system that the learner has created and how the learning was originally stored. Designing the filing system in long-term storage is a *learned* skill and can run the gamut from very loose connections to a highly organized series of networks. Working memory uses a sensory cue that it encodes with the item and files it in a network containing similar items. The cue helps long-term memory locate, identify, and select that item for later retrieval, similar to the way the label on a file folder helps to locate and identify what is in the file. If the learner is recalling a complex

> **Never underestimate the power of transfer. Past learning always influences new learning.**

concept, information has to come from various storage areas to a convergence zone for assembly, verification, and decoding into working memory. Many factors in a learning system affect the nature of this transfer process. Hunter and others have identified four: similarity, critical attributes, association, and the context and degree of original learning. No factor is more important than the others, and they often work together.

Similarity

Transfer is generated by the similarity of the situation in which something is being learned and the situation to which that learning may transfer. Thus, behavior in one environment tends to transfer to other environments that are similar. For example, commercial jet pilots are first trained in flight simulators before they sit in the cockpit of the actual plane. All the training and learnings they acquired in the simulator, an exact replica of the actual plane, will transfer to the real flying situation. This positive transfer helps the pilot get accustomed quickly to the actual plane, and it reduces errors.

If you have ever rented a car, you realize that it does not take you very long to get accustomed to it and drive away. The environment is similar, so most of the important components are in the same places they are in your own car. You may need a few moments, however, to locate the windshield wiper and light switches.

Teachers often use similarity when introducing new material. They may have students learn words with similar spelling patterns, such as *beat, heat, meat,* and *neat.* Students may use their skills at finding locations on a road map to help place ordered numbers on a graph grid. Other examples are fire and tornado drills. Even giving students major tests in the room where they learned the material being tested uses similarity of the environment for positive transfer.

Similarity of sensory modes is another form of transfer. Red representing danger can alert us to traffic lights, the location of fire alarm boxes, or hazardous areas. Sensory similarity can also cause error. Students may confuse *there, their,* and *they're* because they sound alike, or may not be able to pronounce *read* until they know the word's context.

The more specific the cue that working memory attaches to a new learning, the easier it is for long-term memory to identify the item being sought. This process leads to an interesting phenomenon regarding long-term storage and retrieval: **We file by similarity; we retrieve by difference**. That is, long-term memory files new learnings into a network that contains learnings with similar characteristics or associations, as perceived by the learner. This network identification is one of the connections made in working memory during rehearsal and closure. To retrieve an item, long-term memory identifies how it is *different* from all the other items in that network (Figure 4.2).

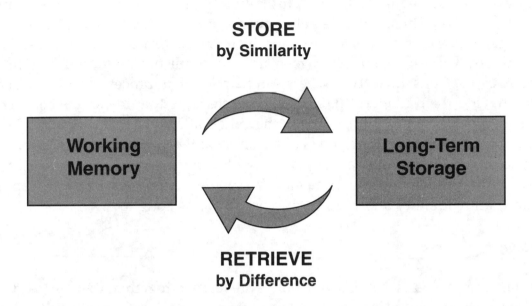

STORE
by Similarity

Working Memory

Long-Term Storage

RETRIEVE
by Difference

Figure 4.2. We tend to store information in networks by similarity, but retrieve it back into working memory by difference.

A simple example is: How would you recognize your best friend in a crowd? It is not because he has two arms, two legs, a head, and a torso. These characteristics make him *similar* to all the others. Rather, it is his *differences,* such as facial features, walk, and voice, that allow you to distinguish him from everyone else. His unique characteristics are called his *critical attributes.* If your friend is an identical twin, however, you might have difficulty picking him out from his brother

> **Two concepts that are very similar to each other ordinarily should not be taught at the same time.**

if both are in the crowd. Similarly, the high degree of similarity between two concepts, coupled with few differences, makes it difficult for the learner to tell them apart. Take, for example, the concepts of latitude and longitude. The similarities between these two ideas far outweigh their differences. Both use identical units of measure, deal with all four compass points, are imaginary lines, locate points on the Earth's surface, and are similar in sound and spelling. Their only real difference is their orientation in space. Teaching them together will be very difficult because their many similarities obscure their singular difference.

Critical Attributes

Critical attributes, characteristics that make one idea unique from all others, are the cues of *difference* that learners can use as part of their storage process. Statements like *Amphibians live both on land and in water, Homonyms are words that sound alike but have dif-*

ferent meanings, and *To produce sound, something must vibrate* are examples of identifying critical attributes.

Identifying the critical attributes of a concept is not an easy task. We live in a culture driven by a quest for equality for all. This culture places a higher value on similarities than on differences. Thus, our cerebral networks are organized around similarity from an early age, and teachers readily use similarity in the classroom to introduce new ideas. Successful retrieval from mental storage areas is accomplished by identifying differences among concepts. Consequently, teachers can help learners process new learnings accurately by having them identify the unique characteristics that make one concept different from all others. For example, what are the critical attributes of an explorer? Will these attributes help to separate Vasco da Gama from Napoleon? Students can use critical attributes to sort concepts so that they are stored in logical networks with appropriate cues. This will facilitate long-term memory's searches and increase the probability that it will accurately identify and retrieve the concept being sought.

Association

Whenever two events, actions, or feelings are learned together, they are said to be *associated,* or bonded, so that the recall of one prompts the spontaneous recall of the other. The word *Romeo* elicits *Juliet,* and *Batman* gets *Robin.* A song you hear being played at a mall may elicit memories of some event that are associated with that song. The odor of a cologne once worn by a close friend from the past triggers the emotions of that relationship. Trademarks and product symbols, such as McDonald's golden arches, are designed to recall the product. Although there is no similarity between the two items, they were learned together and are, therefore, recalled together.

Here is a simple example of transfer. Look at the words listed below. On the lines to the right, write one or two words that come to mind as you read each word in the list.

Monday   _____ _____
dentist   _____ _____
Mom   _____ _____
vacation   _____ _____
babies   _____ _____
emergency   _____ _____
money   _____ _____
Sunday   _____ _____

What you wrote down represents thoughts that you have associated with each word in the list. Here are some responses that others have written for Monday: *work, blues, quarterback, beginning.* For Mom, others have written: *love, apple pie, caring, important, security, dad.* Were your words anything like these? Maybe they were, or maybe not. Show the list to your family and friends and note their responses. Each of us makes different connections with concepts based on our unique experiences; this activity points out the variety of associations that different people can make with the same thought.

Making associations expands the brain's ability to retain information. New connections are formed between neurons and new insights are encoded. Much like a tree growing new branches, everything we remember becomes another set of branches to which memories can be attached. The more we retain, the more we *can* retain.

Association is particularly powerful when feelings or emotions are associated with a learning. We mentioned earlier that the brain's amygdala encodes emotional messages when they are strong and bonds them to learnings for long-term storage. We also noted that emotions usually have a higher priority than cognitive processing for commanding our attention. Words like *abortion, holocaust,* and *capital punishment* often evoke strong feelings. Math anxiety is an example of a strong feeling (probably failure) associated with mathematics. Some students will avoid new situations involving learning mathematics to avoid the negative feelings that are recalled with the content. On the other hand, people devote hours to their hobbies because they associate feelings of pleasure and success with the activity. Thus, teachers should strive to bond positive feelings to new learnings so that students feel competent and can enjoy the process.

Context and Degree of Original Learning

The quality of transfer that occurs during new learning is largely dependent on the quality of the original learning. Most of us can recall easily our social security number or even a poem we learned in our early school years. If the original learning was well-learned and accurate, its influence on new learning will be more constructive and help the student toward greater achievement. Students who did not learn the scientific method well will not be very effective in laboratory analysis, and they will not be able to transfer this learning to future success.

> **Today's learning is tomorrow's transfer. Therefore, if something is worth teaching, it is worth teaching well.**

If something is worth teaching, it is worth teaching well. If we teach students to be conscious of both the new learning and the context into which it fits, we are helping them forge strong associations for future recall. When using transfer, we ask students to bring learnings from their past forward to today. If the past learning was taught well, it should help the students acquire today's learning. What is taught today becomes past learning tomorrow. If it is taught well today, the positive transfer will enhance tomorrow's learning, and so forth. In other words, today's learning is tomorrow's transfer.

Teaching for Transfer

Teachers should not assume that transfer will automatically occur after students acquire a sufficient base of information. Significant and efficient transfer occurs only if we teach to achieve it. Hunter (1982), Perkins and Salomon (1988), and others have suggested that when teachers understand the factors that affect transfer, they can plan lessons that use the power of positive transfer to help students learn faster, solve problems, and generate creative and artistic products that enrich the learning experience.

To teach for transfer, we need to consider two major factors: The time sequence and the complexity of the transfer link between the learnings. The time sequence refers to the way the teacher will use time and transfer in the learning situation. Transfer can occur from past to present or from present to future.

Transfer from Past to Present

In this, the teacher links something from the learner's past that helps add sense and meaning to the new learning. It is important to select an experience that is clear, unambiguous, and closely relevant (not just related) to the new learning. Some examples are:

Past Learning ⟶ *Helps in* ⟶ *Present Learning*

1. An English teacher uses *West Side Story* to introduce *Romeo and Juliet* so that students transfer their knowledge about street gangs and feuds to help them understand Shakespeare's plot.

2. A science teacher asks students to recall what they have learned about plant cells to study the similarities and differences in animal cells.

3. A social studies teacher asks students to think of the causes of the U.S. Civil War to see if they can also explain the causes of the Vietnam War.

Transfer from Present to Future

The teacher makes the present learning situation as similar as possible to a future situation to which the new learning should transfer. For the transfer to be successful, students must attain a high degree of original (current) learning and be able to recognize the critical attributes and concepts that make the situations similar and different:

Present Learning ⟶ *Helps in* ⟶ *Future Learning*

1. Students learn the critical attributes of fact and opinion so they can transfer that learning in the future when evaluating advertising, news reports, election campaigns, and the like.

2. Students learn how to read graphs, pie charts, and tables so that in the future they can evaluate data presented to them for analysis and action.

3. Students learn safe personal and interpersonal hygiene practices to protect their health throughout their lives.

Teaching techniques such as *bridging* and *hugging* are designed to help students make transfer links from past to present and to the future. Examples of these techniques are found in the **Practitioner's Corner** at the end of this chapter.

Complexity of the Link Between Learnings

The way that transfer occurs during a learning situation can range from a very superficial similarity to a sophisticated, abstract association. For example, when renting a car, it takes just a few minutes to get accustomed to the model, find the windshield wiper and light controls, and drive off. Interpreting a pie chart in the school budget requires the recall of graph analysis skills from a prior mathematics course. The new learning environments are perceived as being *similar* to others that the learner has practiced, and that similarity automatically triggers the same learned behaviors.

Metaphor, Analogy, and Simile. The transfer connection can also be much more complex, requiring the learner to make an abstract application of knowledge and skills to the new situation. Metaphors, analogies, and similes are useful devices for promoting abstract transfer. The *metaphor* is the application of a word or phrase to an object or concept that it does not literally denote to suggest a comparison with another object or concept. A person may say, "It's raining cats and dogs outside. I'm drowned!" Obviously, it is not raining animals and the person did not drown. He is speaking figuratively and the metaphor compares things that are essentially dissimilar. An *analogy* compares partial similarity between two things, such as comparing a heart to a pump. The *simile* compares two unlike things: *She is like a rose.*

> **Metaphors can convey meaning of abstract material as well and as rapidly as literal language.**

Metaphors can often convey meaning of abstract material as well and as rapidly as literal language. Metaphors help to explain complex concepts or processes. A geologist explains the movement of glaciers as flowing like batter on a griddle, and that the glacier was an enormous plow upon the land. Comparing life to taking a long trip also is a metaphor. We ask the learner to reflect on how the situations encountered on the road compare to those encountered in life. How can the meaning of bumps, detours, road signs and billboards, places we visited, passed through, or stayed in for a while all compare to life situations? Complex transfer patterns can reach back to the past: *How does the thinking strategy I used when I encountered a major detour help me to decide what course to choose in life now?* It can also transfer to the future: *The planning I used in preparing for the trip should help me prepare for other major decisions I need to make in my life that require extensive planning.*

> **The quality of learning rarely exceeds the quality of teaching.**

These strategies are rich in imagery and enhance the thinking process by encouraging students to seek out associations and connections that they would not ordinarily make (See more in Chapter 5 on imagery). They gain insights into relationships among ideas that help to forge a more thorough understanding of new learning.

Transfer and Constructivism

The proper and frequent use of transfer greatly enhances the constructivist approach to learning. Among the characteristics that Brooks and Brooks (1993) use to describe constructivist teachers are those who: (1) use student responses to alter their instructional strategies and content, (2) foster student dialogue, (3) question student understanding before sharing their own, (4) encourage students to elaborate on their initial responses, and (5) allow students time to construct relationships and create metaphors.

All these characteristics have been discussed here and in previous chapters, and are characteristic of teachers who are proficient in using transfer deliberately throughout their lessons.

PRACTITIONER'S CORNER

Teaching Concepts That Are Very Similar: Avoiding Negative Transfer

Teachers often use similarity to introduce new topics. They say, "You already learned something about this topic when we ... " This is a useful way for students to use positive transfer by recalling similar items from long-term storage that can assist in learning new information.

Similarity, however, can also be a problem. Whenever two concepts have more similarities than differences, such as latitude and longitude, mitosis and meiosis, or simile and metaphor, there is a high risk that the learner will not be able to tell them apart. In effect, the similarities overwhelm the differences, resulting in the learner attaching the same retrieval cues to both concepts. Thus, when the learner uses that cue later to retrieve information, it could produce either or both concepts and the learner may not recognize which is correct.

How To Deal with This Problem. When planning a lesson with two very similar concepts, write down their similarities and differences. If the number of similarities is about the same as the number of differences, there is less chance the students will be confused, but if the number of similarities is far greater than the differences, confusion is likely. In that case, try the following:

- **Teach the Two Concepts at Different Times.** Teach the first concept; make sure that the students thoroughly understand it and can practice it correctly. Then teach a related concept to give the first concept time to be consolidated accurately and fully into long-term storage. Teach the second concept a few weeks later. Now information from the first concept acts for positive transfer in learning the second concept.

- **Teach the Difference(s) First.** Another option is to start by teaching the difference(s) between the two concepts. This works better with older students since they have enough prior learnings to recognize subtle differences. For example, teach that the only real difference between latitude and longitude is their orientation in space. Focusing on and practicing the difference gives learners the warnings and the cues they need to separate the two similar concepts and identify them individually and correctly in the future.

PRACTITIONER'S CORNER

Identifying Critical Attributes for Accurate Transfer

Critical attributes are characteristics that make one concept *unique* among all others. Teachers need to help students identify these attributes so students can use them for eventual and accurate retrieval. Hunter (1982) suggested a five-step process:

1. **Identify the Critical Attributes.** Suppose the learning objective is for the students to understand how mammals are different from all other animals. The two critical attributes of mammals are that (a) they nurse their young through mammary glands, and (b) they have hair.

2. **Teacher Gives Simple Examples.** Next, the teacher gives some simple examples, such as the hamster, human being, cat, dog, and gerbil, to establish the concept. The teacher should give the examples at this point, not the students. Since this new learning is occurring in prime-time when retention is highest, the examples must be correct.

3. **Teacher Gives Complex Examples.** Now the teacher gives more complex examples, such as the porpoise and whale which, unlike most mammals, live in water. It is important here to show how the critical attributes apply.

4. **Students Give Examples.** Here the teacher checks for student understanding to ensure that the critical attributes are used correctly and that the concept is firmly in place.

5. **Teach the Limits of the Critical Attributes.** The learner must recognize that critical attributes may have limits and not apply in every instance. In this lesson, these attributes will accurately identify all mammals, but may incorrectly identify some non-mammals. There is a small group of animals called platypuses which exhibit not only mammalian characteristics, but also those of amphibians and birds. They are in a separate classification.

Take each major concept you teach and identify its critical attributes. Use the five-step process above to help you and the students clearly recognize what makes this concept *different* from all others. These attributes will become valuable cues that students use to increase their understanding as well as the accuracy and rate of retrieval. See the next page for more examples.

PRACTITIONER'S CORNER

Identifying Critical Attributes for Accurate Transfer – Continued

By identifying the critical attributes, the student learns how one concept is different from all other similar concepts. This leads to clearer understanding, concept attainment, the ability to relate the new concept properly to others, and the likelihood that it will be stored and remembered accurately. All subject areas have major concepts whose critical attributes should be clearly identified. Here are a few simple examples:

Social Studies

Law — Made by a government entity, used for the control of behavior, policed, penalty if broken.

Culture — The common behavior of a large group of people who can be identified by specific foods, clothing, art, religion, and music.

Science

Mammal — An animal that has hair and mammary glands.

Planet — A natural heavenly body that revolves around a star, rotates on its axis, and does not produce its own light.

Mathematics

Triangle — A two-dimensional figure, closed, with three sides.

Prime — An integer, value greater than 1, only positive factors are itself and 1.

Language Arts

Sonnet — A poem of 14 lines, meter is iambic pentameter, with a specific rhyming pattern.

Simile — A figure of speech that compares two unlike things.

PRACTITIONER'S CORNER

Teaching for Transfer – Bridging

Teachers can design instructional strategies to promote transfer. Perkins and Salomon (1988), among others, have suggested various techniques for teachers to use to achieve positive transfer. In the technique called *bridging*, the teacher invokes transfer by helping students see the connection and abstraction from what the learner knows to other new learnings and contexts. There are many ways this can be accomplished. Here are a few:

- **Brainstorming.** When introducing a new topic, ask students to brainstorm ways they see this new learning being applied in other situations. For example, what are ways that students can use the skills they have just learned in analyzing charts, tables, and graphs? How else can they use their understandings about the law of supply and demand? What future value is there in knowing about nuclear power generation and alternative energy sources?

- **Analogies.** After learning a topic, use an analogy to examine the similarities and differences between one system and another. For example, ask students to make comparisons: How was the post-Vietnam War period in Vietnam similar to and different from the post-U.S. Civil War period? How is the post-Soviet Union period in Russia today similar to and different from the U.S. post-Revolutionary War period?

- **Metacognition.** When solving problems, ask the students to investigate ways of approaching the solutions and discussing the advantages and disadvantages of each. For example, what solutions are there to meet the increased demand for electrical power in a densely-populated area? What power sources could be used and which would be safest, most economical, most practical, etc.? What are the ways in which governments could regionalize to improve their effectiveness and economy of services? What are the advantages and disadvantages of regionalization? What impact does it have on local government and the democratic process? After applying their solutions, the students discuss how well their approaches worked and how they might change their approaches next time to improve their success. (See more on metacognition in Chapter 6.)

PRACTITIONER'S CORNER

Teaching for Transfer – Hugging

Another technique suggested by Perkins and Salomon (1988) is called *hugging*. This method uses similarity to enhance positive transfer. Hugging strives to make the new learning situation more like future situations to which transfer is desired. This is a lower form of transfer and relies on an almost automatic response from the learner when the new situation is encountered. Teachers can find these connections to similarity in many ways. The key is to make sure that the similarity of situation actually involves the student using the skill or knowledge to be transferred. When students use a word search puzzle to identify certain French verbs written forward or backward, this does not mean that they will be able to understand these verbs in written or spoken French. Hugging means keeping the new instruction as close as possible to the environment and requirements that the students will encounter in the future. Here are a few ways to design hugging:

- **Simulation Games**. These are useful in helping students practice new roles in diverse situations. Debates, mock trials, and investigating labor disputes are ways that students can experiment with various approaches to solving complex legal and social issues.

- **Mental Practice.** When a student is not able to replicate an upcoming situation, it is very useful for the student to mentally practice what that situation could be like. The student reviews potential variations of the situation and devises mental strategies for dealing with the different scenarios. Suppose a student is to interview a political candidate for the school newspaper. In addition to the prepared questions, what other questions could the student ask, depending on the candidate's response? What if the candidate is reticent, or changes the course of the questioning?

- **Contingency Learning.** Here the learner asks what other information or skill must be acquired to solve a problem successfully, and learns it. If the student is building a model to demonstrate gas laws, what else must the student learn to design and construct the apparatus at a reasonable cost so that it shows the desired gas relationships effectively? Learning these contingent skills in the context of solving another problem is much more effective than learning them in any other way.

PRACTITIONER'S CORNER

Using Metaphors To Enhance Transfer

Metaphors can convey meaning as well and as rapidly as literal language. They are usually rich in imagery, are useful bridging strategies, and can apply to both content and skill learnings. West, Farmer, and Wolff (1991) suggest a six-step process for using metaphors in lesson design:

1. **Select the Metaphor.** The criteria for selecting the appropriate metaphor center on goodness of fit (how well the metaphor explains the target concept or process), degree or richness of imagery, familiarity that the students will have with it, and its novelty.

2. **Emphasize the Metaphor.** The metaphor must be emphasized consistently throughout the lesson. Students should be alerted to interpret the metaphor figuratively and not literally.

3. **Establish Context.** Proper interpretation of the metaphor requires that the teacher establish the context for its use. Metaphors should not be used in isolation, especially if the students lack the background to understand them.

4. **Provide Instructions for Imagery.** Teachers should provide students with the instructions they will need to benefit from the rich imagery usually present in metaphors. "Form a mental picture of this" is good advice. (See the **Practitioner's Corner** on imagery in the next chapter.)

5. **Emphasize Similarities and Differences.** Because the metaphor juxtaposes the similarities of one known object or procedure with another, teachers should emphasize the similarities and differences between the metaphor and the new learning.

6. **Provide Opportunities for Rehearsal.** Use rote and elaborate rehearsal strategies to help students recognize the similarities and differences between the metaphor and the new learning, and to enhance their depth of understanding and types of associations.

CHAPTER 5 _____

LEFT/RIGHT BRAIN PROCESSING: WHAT'S ALL THE FUSS ABOUT?

Normal people have not half a brain nor two brains, but one gloriously differentiated brain, with each hemisphere contributing its specialized abilities.

— Jerre Levy,
Right Brain, Left Brain: Fact and Fiction

Chapter Highlights: This chapter explores the research on how the two hemispheres of the brain process information, and debunks some myths that have obscured the value of this work. You will be able to determine whether you have a hemispheric dominance and what that means about how you learn and think. The chapter also examines the implications of this research for classroom instruction and for the curriculum and structure of schools.

During the late 1950s, neurosurgeons decided that the best way to help patients with severe epileptic seizures was to sever the corpus callosum (Figure 1.1), the thick cable of nerve fibers that connects the two cerebral hemispheres. This last-ditch approach would isolate the hemispheres so that seizures in the damaged hemisphere would not travel to the other side. The surgery had been tried on monkeys with epilepsy and the results were encouraging. By the early 1960s, surgeons were ready to try the technique on human beings. One of the pioneers was Dr. Roger Sperry of the California Institute of Technology. Between 1961 and 1969, surgeons Joseph Bogen and Phillip Vogel successfully performed several of these operations under Sperry's guidance. Although the operations resulted in a substantial reduction or elimination of the seizures, no one was sure what effect cutting this bridge between the hemispheres would have on these "split-brain" patients.

Sperry and his student Michael Gazzaniga conducted a series of experiments with these patients and made a remarkable discovery.[10] Splitting the brain seemed to result in two separate domains of awareness. When a pencil was placed in the left hand (controlled by the right hemisphere) of a blindfolded patient, the patient could not name it. When the pencil was shifted to the right hand, however, the patient named it

> **The left and right hemispheres of the brain have some distinctly different functions that are not easily interchangeable.**

instantly. Neither hemisphere seemed to know what the other was doing and they acted, as Sperry said, "each with its own memory and will, competing for control."

As the tests progressed, Sperry charted the characteristics each hemisphere displayed. He concluded that each hemisphere "seems to have its own separate and private sensations; its own perceptions; its own impulses to act, with related volitional, cognitive and learning experiences." This research showed that the right and left hemispheres had distinctly different functions that are not readily interchangeable. It also solved the mystery of the corpus callosum. Its purpose is largely to unify awareness and allow the two hemispheres to share memory and learning. Sperry won the 1981 Nobel Prize in medicine for this work.

Left and Right Hemisphere Processing

Continued testing of split-brain patients revealed considerable consistency in the different ways the two halves of the brain store and process information (Figure 5.1). This cerebral specialization is called *hemisphericity*.

Left Hemisphere. The left brain is the *logical* hemisphere. It monitors the areas for speech, reading, and writing. It is analytical and evaluates factual material in a rational way. It understands the literal interpretation of words, and detects time and sequence. It recognizes words, letters, and numbers.

Right Hemisphere. The right brain is the *intuitive* hemisphere. It gathers information more from images than words. It looks for patterns and can process many kinds of information simultaneously. It interprets language through context—body language and tone of voice—rather than through literal meanings. It specializes in spatial perception and is capable of fantasy and creativity. It recognizes places, faces, and objects.

Continuing research on the kind of processing done by each hemisphere has expanded our understanding of this remarkable division of labor. The chart on p. 88 summarizes these and other functions that the hemispheres seem to perform as they deal with the vast amount of new and past information that must be assessed every second.

---

10. These experiments were detailed in an article by Michael Gazzaniga in "The Split Brain in Man," *Scientific American*, August 1967, pp. 24–29.

LEFT SIDE:

Speech
Analysis
Time
Sequence

Recognizes:

Words
Letters
Numbers

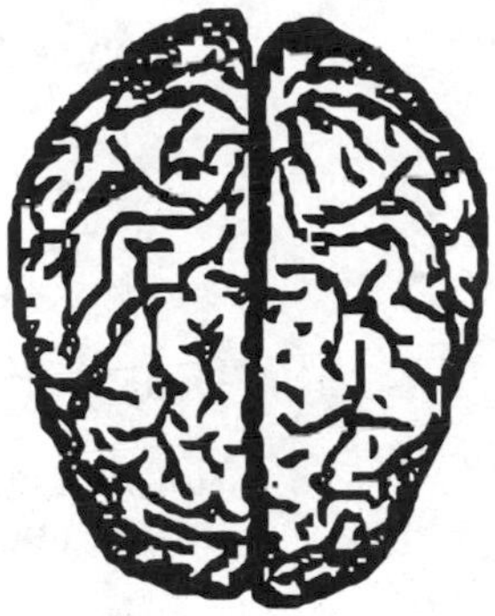

RIGHT SIDE:

Creativity
Patterns
Spatial
Context

Recognizes:

Faces
Places
Objects

Figure 5.1. *The left and right hemispheres of the human brain process information differently.*

In a normal individual, the results of the separate processing are exchanged with the opposite hemisphere through the corpus callosum. There is harmony in their goals and they complement each other in almost all activities. Thus, the individual benefits from the integration of the processing done by each hemisphere and is afforded greater comprehension of the situation that initiated the processing.

Hemispheric Dominance

Since the work of Sperry, case studies and additional testing procedures (Gazzaniga, 1989) have enabled researchers to understand more about the functions of each hemisphere. These tests include anesthetizing one hemisphere, PET scans, electroencephalographs (which record electrical impulses), and hemisphere-specific vision and hearing tests. The research has shown that most people have a dominant hemisphere, and that this dominance affects personality, abilities, and learning style. The dominance runs the gamut from neutral (no preference) to strongly left or right. Those who are left-hemisphere dominant tend to be more verbal, analytical, and good problem solvers. Right-hemisphere dominant individuals paint and draw well, are good at math, and deal with the visual world more easily than with the verbal.

The dominance of either hemisphere does not mean that we do not use both hemispheres; it suggests that when we are faced with a task that requires a good deal of thought, we tend to shift to the dominant hemisphere. In a simple task, we use the hemisphere that will accomplish it more efficiently.

Examples of Dominance

Suppose you are right-handed. A pen is on the table just next to your *left* hand, and someone asks you to pass the pen. Since this is a simple task, you will pick it up with

LEFT HEMISPHERE FUNCTIONS	RIGHT HEMISPHERE FUNCTIONS
Connected to right side of the body.	Connected to left side of the body.
Deals with inputs one at a time.	Integrates many inputs at once.
Processes information in a linear and sequential manner.	Processes information more diffusely and simultaneously.
Deals with time.	Deals with space.
Responsible for verbal expression and language.	Responsible for gestures, facial movements, and body language.
Responsible for invariable and arithmetic operations.	Responsible for relational and mathematical operations.
Specializes in recognizing words and numbers.	Specializes in recognizing places, faces, objects, and music.
Does logical and analytical thinking.	Does intuitive and holistic thinking.
The seat of reason.	The seat of passion and dreams.
Crucial side for wordsmiths and engineers.	Crucial side for artists, craftspeople, and musicians.

your left hand in a smooth motion and pass it. You are not likely to stretch your right hand across your body, twist your torso, and hand over the pen. If the person asks you to throw the pen, however, you will probably use your right hand since this task is more difficult. We shift to our dominant hemisphere as the thinking becomes more complex.

During learning, both hemispheres are engaged, processing the information or skill according to their specializations and exchanging the results with the opposite hemisphere through the corpus callosum. Just as if someone were to toss a pen to you, your likelihood of successfully catching it would increase greatly if you used *both* hands to catch it, not just the right (dominant) hand.

Knowing the difference between how the left and right hemispheres process information explains why we succeed with some

> **Most people have a dominant hemisphere. This dominance affects their personality, abilities, and learning style.**

tasks but not with others, especially when we are trying to do them simultaneously. Most of us can carry on a conversation (left hemisphere activity) while driving a car (right hemisphere activity). In this case, each task is controlled by different hemispheres, but trying to carry on a conversation on the telephone while talking to someone in the room at the same time is very difficult since they are functions of the same (left) hemisphere and interfere with each other.

Testing Your Own Hemispheric Dominance

There are many instruments available to help individuals assess their hemispheric dominance. The one below takes just a few minutes. The results are only an indication of your dominance and are not conclusive. You should use additional instruments to collect more data before reaching any conclusion about your hemispheric dominance.

Directions: From each pair below, circle A or B corresponding to the sentence that **best describes you**. Answer all questions. There are no right or wrong answers.

1. A. I prefer to find my own way of doing a new task.
    B. I prefer to be told the best way to do a new task.

2. A. I have to make my own plans.
    B. I can follow anyone's plans.

3. A. I am a very flexible and unpredictable person.
    B. I am a very stable and consistent person.

4. A. I keep everything in a particular place.
    B. Where I keep things depends on what I am doing.

5. A. I spread my work evenly over the time I have.
    B. I prefer to do my work at the last minute.

6. A. I know I am right because I have good reasons.
    B. I know when I am right, even without reasons.

7. A. I need a lot of variety and change in my life.
    B. I need a well-planned and orderly life.

8. A. I sometimes have too many ideas in a new situation.
    B. I sometimes don't have any ideas in a new situation.

9. A. I do easy things first and the important things last.
    B. I do the important things first and the easy things last.

10. A. I choose what I **know** is right when making a hard decision.
    B. I choose what I **feel** is right when making a hard decision.

11. A. I plan my time for doing my work.
    B. I don't think about the time when I work.

12. A. I usually have good self-discipline.
    B. I usually act on my feelings.

13. A. Other people don't understand how I organize things.
    B. Other people think I organize things well.

14. A. I agree with new ideas before other people do.
    B. I question new ideas more than other people do.

15. A. I tend to think more in **pictures**.
    B. I tend to think more in **words**.

16. A. I try to find the one best way to solve a problem.
    B. I try to find different ways to solve a problem.

17. A. I can usually **analyze** what is going to happen next.
    B. I can usually **sense** what is going to happen next.

18. A. I am not very imaginative in my work.
    B. I use my imagination in nearly everything I do.

19. A. I begin many jobs that I never finish.
    B. I finish a job before starting a new one.

20. A. I look for new ways to do old jobs.
    B. When one way works well, I don't change it.

21. A. It is fun to take risks.
    B. I have fun without taking risks.

Scoring:

Count the number of "A" responses to questions 1, 3, 7, 8, 9, 13, 14, 15, 19, 20, and 21. Place that number on the line to the right.

A. _____

Count the number of "B" responses to the remaining questions. Place that number on the line to the right.

B. _____

Total the "A" and "B" responses you counted.

Total _____

The total indicates your hemispheric dominance according to the following scale:

0–5	Strong left hemisphere dominance
6–8	Moderate left hemisphere dominance
9–12	Bilateral hemisphere balance (little or no dominance)
13–15	Moderate right hemisphere dominance
16–21	Strong right hemisphere dominance

Cautions About Hemispheric Dominance

While there is a substantial body of evidence that each hemisphere has its specialized abilities, we should not jump to the conclusion that normal people have two brains or are only functioning with half a brain. The differences are not all-or-nothing. Quite the contrary, normal people have one integrated and magnificently differentiated brain that generates a single mind and self. However, misinformation about the specialization of the hemispheres and several popular myths persist.

Specialization of the Hemispheres

The research data support the notion that each hemisphere has its own set of functions in information processing and thinking, but these functions are not *exclusive* to only one hemisphere. Here is what the research is uncovering:

- Logic is not confined to the left hemisphere. Some patients with right-brain damage fail to see the lack of logic in their thinking when they propose to take a walk even when they are completely paralyzed.

- Creativity or intuition are not solely in the right hemisphere. Creativity can remain, though diminished, even after extensive right hemisphere damage.

- Since the two hemispheres do not function independently, it is impossible to educate only one hemisphere in a normal brain.

- Specialization does not mean exclusivity. There is no evidence that people are purely left or right brained. One hemisphere may be more active in most people, but only in varying degrees.

- Finally, one hemisphere can take over the jobs of the other when the latter is severely damaged or surgically removed. Although the two are specialized in the normal brain, each one seems to retain the capabilities of the whole brain.

The Myths About Hemispheric Dominance

Several myths connecting hemispheric dominance to other variables have evolved and endured during the past two decades. The myths have obscured the benefit of this research and undermined its value to the teaching/learning process. Here are three common myths we can debunk.

Handedness (lateral dominance). Because the hemispheres of the brain control the opposite sides of the body, there has been much speculation that hemispheric dominance is directly connected to handedness, or lateral dominance. While there is some evidence that more right-hemisphere preferred individuals are left-handed than right-handed, there is no direct cause-and-effect connection between handedness and hemispheric dominance. Thus, it is incorrect to assume that most right-handed people are left-hemisphere dominant and vice versa.

Intelligence. There is no research to support the notion that those with one hemispheric dominance are any more or less intelligent than those with the opposite dominance. Individuals who are strongly and oppositely dominant will exhibit vastly different personalities and learning styles, but this has no connection to intelligence as we have defined it or the ability to learn.

Genetics. There is no evidence that hemispheric dominance is inherited. Studies of several generations of many families show mixed, unpredictable dominance. This lack of a genetic connection is important as psychologists look for causes of hemisphericity.

Test Question No. 10: *Intelligence is strongly connected to whether people have left or right brain dominance.*

Answer: *False. Left and right brain hemisphere dominance has no link to intelligence.*

The Gender Connection

Is there any variable connected to hemispheric dominance? Studies begun in the early 1970s by Jerre Levy at the University of Chicago, and repeated since in different locations, have shown a gender connection. Females perform better on tests of perceptual speed, verbal fluency, determining the placement of objects (sequence), identifying specific attributes of objects, precision manual tasks, and arithmetic calculations. Males perform better on spatial tasks, such as mentally rotating three-dimensional objects, at target-directed motor skills, spotting shapes embedded in complex diagrams, and in mathematical reasoning. The brains of the two sexes are subtly but significantly different. In general, although there is a great deal of overlap, Shaywitz et al. (1995) and Gur (1995) have shown through PET scans and functional MRIs that males and females use different areas of their brains when accomplishing similar tasks. These and other studies further indicate that more females are left-hemisphere dominant and more males are right-hemisphere dominant. While no one knows for sure why this is so, there are several theories that attempt to explain these results.

The Hormone Theory. One possibility is that hormones, such as testosterone and androgen, influence brain development differently in the sexes. Testosterone seems to delay the development of the left hemisphere in boys. Thus, girls get a head start in using the left hemisphere; boys are forced to rely more on their right hemisphere. The early exposure to these hormones seems to alter other brain functions (such as language acquisition and spatial perception) permanently for the individual.

The Natural Selection Theory. A related theory suggests that natural selection affected our brain characteristics as we evolved. For thousands of years, the division of labor between the sexes was distinct. In prehistoric times, men were responsible for hunting large game over long distances, making weapons, and defending the group from predators, animal and otherwise. Women took care of the home and the children, prepared food, and made clothing. Such specialization required different cerebral operations from men and woman. Men needed more route-finding, spatial abilities, and better targeting skills; women needed more fine motor and timing skills to maintain the household.

> **More girls than boys are left hemisphere dominant; more boys than girls are right hemisphere dominant. The reasons are not as important as our response.**

The Environment Theory. Another prevailing theory looks to a combination of the different ways the sexes develop and interact with their environment as an explanation. First, studies of infant boys and girls demonstrate that the acuity of senses does not develop identically in both genders. Hearing and touch (left-hemisphere controlled) develop more quickly in girls than boys. Sight (right-hemisphere controlled), however, develops more rapidly in boys. Second, parents tend to treat baby boys differently from baby girls. And third, studies show that boys and girls between the ages of 6 and 12 spend their out-of-school time quite differently as they are growing up. Girls are more likely to spend their free time indoors. In this structured environment, girls play with dolls and develop language talking with them, they are exposed to more language through radio and television, and they are more conscious of time because of clocks, media, and other family members coming home. This environment, psychologists argue, promotes left hemisphere dominance.

On the other hand, more boys spend their free time outdoors. In this unstructured environment, boys rely more on space (location) than time, design their own games, use more visual than verbal skills during play, and use little language and only in context to accomplish a task. This behavior promotes right-hemisphere dominance. Taken together, the theories and evidence suggest that the brains of males and females are organized differently from very early in their development, leading, among other things, to different preferences in learning.

Regardless of the source of these preferences, we should avoid using hemispheric dominance to stereotype individuals, to assume that one dominance is better than another, or that they cannot accomplish certain tasks because of their dominance. The cause of gender dominance, for all practical purposes, is not relevant. It is our response that really matters. We can use this research to understand better how hemispheric dominance affects learning and what teachers can do about it in their classrooms.

Schools and Hemispheric Dominance

Left Hemisphere Schools?

Take a moment to think about the entire schooling process that takes place from kindergarten through grade 12. During this mental review, look again at the list of left and right hemisphere functions. Is K–12 schooling best described by the characteristics listed for the left hemisphere, the right hemisphere, or both equally? Most educators say predominantly left hemisphere. Schools are structured environments that run according to time schedules, favor facts and rules over patterns, and are largely verbal.

This means that left-hemisphere dominant learners (mainly girls) feel more comfortable in this environment. The stronger the left-hemisphere dominance, the more successful these learners can be. Converse-

> **Most K–12 public schooling tends to favor left hemisphere dominant learners.**

ly, right-hemisphere dominant learners (mainly boys) are not comfortable; the stronger the right-hemisphere dominance, the more hostile the learning environment seems. This could explain why most teachers admit that they have many more discipline problems with boys than with girls. Maybe what this research is saying is that boys (more accurately, right-hemisphere dominant learners) are not born with a "mean gene," but are too often placed in uncomfortable learning environments where they react rebelliously.

Mathematics Anxiety

Girls in high school are much more likely to have anxiety over studying mathematics than boys. Yet, when looking at the specializations of the hemispheres, it would appear at first glance that mathematics requires mostly left hemisphere processing. Actually, it is *arithmetic* (linear, logical, only one answer to each problem) that is left hemisphere centered. Thus, left-hemisphere dominant learners feel comfortable doing arithmetic and gain confidence in those skills through their elementary school grades. Their amygdalae have recorded positive emotional messages of success along with this learning. When they take their first right-hemisphere centered course, however, usually algebra I (holistic, relational, multiple solutions), they begin to have problems and get confused about their competence since they did well in arithmetic.

If they succeed in struggling through algebra I, their reward is geometry, an even more right hemisphere-centered subject! This deterioration of achievement in an area where there was once success leads to tension, helplessness, and a dread of mathematics described as "math anxiety." The amygdalae now encode a different message with this learning—one of frustration and alarm, rather than of success and confidence.

Learning Science

Taught properly, science is a right hemisphere-centered subject since it is a process for collecting information and data and for making inferences based on those data. True science is intuitive, creative, and relational. Sadly, science, especially in elementary schools, is taught too often as fact memorization. Left hemisphere learners do well with this unfortunate approach to science, but they get distraught in courses that focus on science as a holistic process.

Learning a Second Language

Left-right hemisphere processing and dominance seem to play an important role in learning a second language. Danesi (1990) is convinced that strategies that teachers use to foster inter-hemisphere cooperation are essential for helping students acquire a second language. His studies of brain-damaged subjects indicate that grammatical and phonological (sound-related) aspects of language are handled by the left hemisphere. More subtle aspects of speech, such as the ability to interpret sarcasm, hyperbole, and other non-literal meanings, are processed in the right hemisphere. Danesi describes the left hemisphere as the analytic device that processes discrete units of language, while the right hemisphere is a *Gestalt* device that puts the units together into meaningful wholes. In other words, the left hemisphere operates on "texts"; the right hemisphere operates on "context." He laments the observation that schools are over-emphasizing the verbal and analytical skills while neglecting the non-verbal forms of communication that are more likely to lead to deeper understanding of the language and its structure.

The work of Bradshaw and Rogers (1993) supports this hemisphericity approach to second language acquisition. Their studies of patients with hemisphere damage show that the right hemisphere is responsible for speech melody, intonation, accent, and stress, and contributes to such vital linguistic behaviors as fluency of thought and pragmatic understanding.

While there is still no universal agreement on the interpretation of all these findings, there is, nonetheless, a growing recognition of the role of the right hemisphere in learning a second language. Many researchers believe that the right hemisphere is superior in processing new stimuli, that is, stimuli for which the learner has no cognitive experience.

Imagery

For most people, the left hemisphere specializes in coding information verbally while the right hemisphere codes information visually. Although teachers spend much time talking (and sometimes have their students talk) about the learning objective, little time is given to developing visual cues. This process, called imagery, is the mental visualization of objects, events, and arrays related to the new learning, and represents a major way of storing information in the brain. Imagery is different from imagining in that it is specific and focused on the new learning, while imagining has no limits.

A mental image is a pictorial representation of something physical or of an experience. The more information an image contains, the richer it is. Some people are more capable of forming rich images than others, but the research evidence is clear: Individuals can be taught to search their minds for images and be guided through the process to select appropriate images that, through hemispheric integration, enhance learning and increase retention.

Training students in imagery encourages them to search long-term storage for appropriate images and to use them more like a movie than a photograph. For example, one recalls the house one lived in for many years. From the center hall with its gleaming chandelier, one mentally turns left and "walks" through the living room to the sun room beyond. To the right of the hall is the paneled dining room and then the kitchen with the avocado green appliances and oak cabinets. In the back, one sees the flagstone patio, the manicured lawn, and the garden with its variety of flowers. The richness of the image allows one to focus on just a portion of it and generate additional amounts of detail. In this image, one could mentally stop in any room and visualize the furniture and other decor.

Imagery should become a regular part of classroom strategies as early as kindergarten. In the primary grades, the teacher should supply the images to ensure accuracy. Later, teachers should encourage students to form their own images. Research studies (Parrott, 1986) continue to attest to how the power of imagery aids in recalling word associations, visual arrays, prose learning,

> **Imagery should be used regularly in all classrooms to enhance association and recall.**

complex procedures, and motor learning. So much research is being done in this area that there is now a *Journal of Mental Imagery*.

Developing Strategies for Hemisphericity

Does the research on hemisphericity suggest that we should shift our attention in schools away from the left hemisphere and focus only on right hemisphere activities? Of course not. Each hemisphere has capabilities that the other hemisphere lacks, so utilizing *both* during learning enhances understanding. A recent study looked at three ways of teaching children vocabulary. One way is to have the children read and write the definitions; the second is to read the definition and trace a picture of each definition; the third is having the children read the definition and then draw their own picture of the definition. The children remembered the definitions best when they drew their own pictures; that is, when they used a combination of reading the words (left hemisphere) with creating their own picture (right hemisphere).

Teachers, then, need to ensure that their lessons contain activities that stimulate and involve both hemispheres during the learning process. Strategies such as visualized notemaking, concept mapping, imagery, and others (see the **Practitioner's Corners**) are designed to get both hemispheres involved in new learning and to work interactively to enhance meaning, understanding, and retention.

PRACTITIONER'S CORNER

Teaching to Both Hemispheres:
General Guidelines

Although the two hemispheres process information differently, we learn best when both are engaged in learning. Just as we would catch more balls with both hands, we catch more information with both hemispheres processing and integrating the learning. Teachers should design lessons that include activities directed at both hemispheres so that students can integrate the new learning into a meaningful whole. Here are some ways to do that in daily planning:

- **Deal with Concepts Verbally *and* Visually.** When teaching new concepts, alternatively use discussion (left hemisphere) with visual (right hemisphere) models. Write key words on the chalkboard that represent the attributes of the concept being taught, then use a simple diagram to represent relationships among the key ideas within and between concepts. This helps students attach both auditory and visual cues to the new information and increases the likelihood that sense and meaning will emerge. When showing a film or videotape, show the smallest segment with maximum meaning, then stop the tape and discuss what was shown.

  How we position information in a visual aid (overhead transparency, chalkboard, easel pad) indicates the relationships of concepts and ideas, which are processed by the right hemisphere. Vertical positioning tends to imply a sequence or hierarchy. Thus, writing:

  > Delaware
  > Pennsylvania
  > New Jersey

  would be appropriate to indicate the order of their admission into the Union. Writing them horizontally:

  > Delaware, Pennsylvania, New Jersey

  implies a parallel relationship that would be appropriate if we were identifying any three populous eastern states. Teachers should avoid writing information in visual aids in a haphazard way whenever a parallel or hierarchical relationship between or among the information is important for students to remember.

PRACTITIONER'S CORNER

Teaching to Both Hemispheres: General Guidelines – Continued

- **Discuss Concepts Logically and Intuitively.** Concepts should be presented to students from different perspectives that encourage them to use both hemispheres. For example: If you are teaching about the Civil War, talk about the factual (logical) events, such as major causes, battles, and the economic and political impacts. When the students understand these, move on to more thought-provoking (intuitive) activities, such as asking what might have happened if Lincoln had not been assassinated, or what our country might be like now if the Confederate States had won the war.

  After teaching basic concepts in arithmetic, ask students to design a number system to a base other than 10. This is a simple and interesting process that helps students understand the scheme of our decimal number system. In literature, after reading part of a story or play, ask students to write a plausible ending using the facts already presented. In science, after giving some facts about the structure of the periodic table of the elements, ask students to explain how they would experiment with a new element to determine its place in the table.

- **Avoid Conflicting Messages.** Make sure that your words, tone, and pacing match your gestures, facial expressions, and body language. The left hemisphere interprets words literally, but the right hemisphere evaluates body language, tone, and content. If the two hemispheric interpretations are inconsistent, a conflict message is generated. The student withdraws internally to resolve the conflict and is no longer focused on the learning.

- **Design Activities and Assessments for Both Hemispheres.** Students of different hemispheric dominance express themselves in different ways. Give students options in testing and in completing assignments so they can select the option best suited to their learning styles. For example, after completing a major unit on the U.S. Civil War, students could write term papers on particular aspects of the war, draw pictures, create and present plays of important events, or construct models that represent battles, the surrender at Appomattox, etc.

PRACTITIONER'S CORNER

Teaching to Both Hemispheres:
Skills and Strategies for the Left Hemisphere

We learn best when both hemispheres are engaged in learning. Thus, it is useful to know the types of teaching strategies that involve the skills inherent in each hemisphere. Here is a summary of a study done by Key (1991) who collected numerous hemisphere-specific strategies from the research literature. The chapter text helps to explain how the research on hemisphericity supports the strategies listed below. *Remember, however, that we cannot educate just one hemisphere.* Rather, we are ensuring that our daily instruction includes activities that stimulate *both* hemispheres.

Teaching Strategies for Involving Left-Hemisphere Skills

- Organize the class into an efficient workplace. Distribute the talkers around the room; they will spark discussions when needed.

- Organize bulletin boards to be relevant to the current content and easily understood.

- Make clean erasures on the chalkboard. This reduces the chance that previous and unrelated word cues will become associated with the topic under discussion.

- Let students read, write, and compute often to enhance this left hemisphere activity.

- Create and analyze metaphors to enhance meaning and encourage higher-order thinking.

- Stress the importance of being on time. Encourage students to carry agendas.

- Teach students to set study goals for themselves, to stick to their goals, and to reward themselves when they achieve them.

- Ask "what if" questions to encourage logical thinking as they consider all possibilities for solving problems.

PRACTITIONER'S CORNER

Teaching to Both Hemispheres:
Skills and Strategies for the Right Hemisphere

We learn best when both hemispheres are engaged in learning. Thus, it is useful to know the types of teaching strategies that involve the skills inherent in each hemisphere. Here is a summary of a study done by Key (1991) who collected many hemisphere-specific strategies from the research literature. The chapter text helps explain how the research on hemisphericity supports the strategies listed below. *Remember, however, that we cannot educate just one hemisphere.* Rather, we are ensuring that our daily instruction includes activities to stimulate both hemispheres.

Teaching Strategies for Involving Right-Hemisphere Skills

- Give students options and allow them to do oral or written reports. Oral reports allow the right hemisphere to fit concepts together while requiring fewer mechanics than written work.

- Use the chalkboard and overhead projector to show illustrations, cartoons, charts, timelines, and graphs to allow students to visually organize information and relationships.

- Tying lessons together and using proper closure (Chapter 3) allows the brain to compare new information to what has already been learned.

- Allow direct experiences through role playing and simulations.

- Allow students time to interact with each other as they discuss the new learnings.

- Teach students to use generalities and perceptions. Have them use metaphors and similes to make connections between unlike items. This is an important function for future transfer of learning.

- Provide frequent opportunities for hands-on learning. Students need to realize that they must discover and order relationships in the real world.

PRACTITIONER'S CORNER

Teaching to Both Hemispheres: Acquiring a Second Language

Studies by Danesi (1990) and others indicate that the right hemisphere takes the lead in the early stages when an individual is learning a second language. The left hemisphere takes on its share of work in later stages. Thus, teachers of foreign languages and of English as a Second Language (ESL) should:

- **Follow a Right-to-Left Hemisphere Sequence of Strategies.** Gear initial instruction toward intuition and brainstorming and concrete visual strategies. Later, move on to more organizational and formal sequential and verbal instruction.

- **Develop Communication Competence.** One of the primary goals of learning a second language is to gain competence in communication. Becoming a competent communicator in a second language involves acquiring four major competencies that require integration of the verbal and non-verbal aspects of language as well as right and left hemisphere processing. Teachers need to keep these four competencies in mind as they select their instructional strategies:

  Grammatical Competence. The degree to which a student has mastered the formal linguistic code of the language, including vocabulary, rules of punctucation, word formation, and sentence structure. This entails the analytic and sequential processing of the left hemisphere.

  Socio-Linguistic Competence. The ability to use grammatical forms appropriately in contexts that range from very informal to very formal styles. It includes varying the choice of verbal and non-verbal language to adapt the speech to a specific person or social context, and this requires sensitivity to individual and socio-cultural differences. This is essentially the right hemisphere's ability to contextualize language.

  Discourse Competence. The ability to combine form and thought into a coherent expression. It involves knowing how to use conjunctions, adverbs, and transitional phrases to achieve continuity of thought. This requires the integration of both hemispheres; the analytic ability of the left hemisphere to generate the grammatical features, and the right hemisphere to synthesize them into meaningful, coherent wholes.

PRACTITIONER'S CORNER

Teaching to Both Hemispheres: Acquiring a Second Language – Continued

Strategic Competence. The ability to use verbal and non-verbal communication strategies, such as body language and circumlocution, to compensate for the user's imperfect knowledge of the language, and to negotiate meaning. This requires the active participation of both hemispheres to generate verbal and non-verbal strategies to achieve communication.

This research points out the need for teachers to ensure that the non-verbal form of intellect is not neglected in second language acquisition. In planning lessons, teachers should:

- Not rely heavily on grammar, vocabulary memorization, and mechanical translations, especially during the early stages of this instruction.

- Do more with contextual language, trial and error, brainstorming of meaning, visual activities, and role playing.

- Give the right hemisphere its opportunity to establish the contextual networking it needs to grasp meaning and nuance.

This approach also benefits left hemisphere learners by increasing the contributions their right hemispheres make to their language competence. When these skills are in place, shift to more work on enlarging their vocabulary and knowledge of grammar.

PRACTITIONER'S CORNER

Teaching to Both Hemispheres:
Using Imagery

Imagery is a strategy that can run the gamut from simple concrete pictures to complex motor learning and multi-step procedures. Since imagery is still not a common instructional strategy, it should be implemented early and gradually. Here are some guidelines adapted from Parrott (1986) and West, Farmer, and Wolff (1991) for using imagery regularly in instruction. It is a powerful aid to hemisphere integration and retention.

- **Prompting.** Use prompts for telling students to form mental images of the content being learned. They can be as simple as "form a picture in your mind of ... " to more complex directions. Prompts should be specific to the content or task and should be accompanied by relevant photographs, charts, or arrays, especially for younger children.

- **Modeling.** Model imagery by describing your own image to the class and explaining how that image helps your recall and use of the current learning. Modeling a procedure and having the students mentally practice the steps is also effective.

- **Interaction.** Strive for rich, vivid images where items interact. The richer the image, the more information that can be included with it. If there are two or more items in the images, they should be visualized as acting on each other. If the recall is a ball and a bat, for example, imagine the bat hitting the ball.

- **Reinforcement.** Have students talk about the images they formed and get feedback from others on their accuracy, vividness, and interaction.

- **Add Context.** Whenever possible, add context to the interaction to increase retention and recall. For example, if the task is to recall prefixes and suffixes, the context could be a parade with the prefixes in front urging the suffixes in the rear to catch up.

- **Avoid Overloading the Image.** While good images are complete representations of the major item to be remembered, they should not have so many items as to overload the working memory. Remember, working memory has a functional capacity in older students of about seven items.

PRACTITIONER'S CORNER

Teaching to Both Hemispheres: Visualized Notetaking

Visualized notetaking is a strategy that encourages students to associate language with visual imagery. It invokes the left hemisphere's ability to sequence verbal information and combines that on paper with the right hemisphere's skill for generating symbols and holistic visual patterns. Teachers should encourage students to link verbal notes with images and symbols that show sequence, patterns, or relationships. Some examples suggested by Stein (1987) include:

- **Time Line.** <u>Person</u>   <u>Date</u>   <u>Event</u>
  |
  |
  |
  |

Use the Time Line for remembering persons, dates, and events.

- **Stickperson.** Use the stickperson symbol to remember information about a person or group of people. The student attaches notes about a person in eight areas to the appropriate spot on the stick figure: ideas to the brain; hopes/vision to the eyes; words to the mouth; actions to the hands; feelings to the heart; movement to the feet; weaknesses to the Achilles' heel; and strengths to the arm muscle.

- **Expository Visuals.** These take many forms. Use a triangle to help students collect and visualize the cause/effect interrelationships for an event. Causes are written on one leg of the triangle, effects on the other leg. Conclusions that students draw from an analysis of the causes and effects are written on the base. Creating different designs to visualize other topics is a valuable left/right hemisphere activity.

- **Notebook Design.** Even the design of the notebook page can call both hemispheres into play to enhance learning and retention. One variation involves dividing the notebook page into sections for topics, vocabulary, important questions, things to remember, next homework assignment, and next test. Positioning each area on the page acts as a visual organizer that promotes the use of appropriate symbols.

PRACTITIONER'S CORNER

Teaching to Both Hemispheres:
Concept Mapping – General Guidelines

Concept mapping consists of extracting concepts and terms from curriculum content and plotting them visually to show and name the relationships between and among them. This process allows the learner to establish a visual representation (right hemisphere) of relations between concepts that might be presented only verbally (left hemisphere). The integration of visual/verbal enhances understanding of concepts whether they be abstract, concrete, verbal, or non-verbal. The key to the value of concept mapping is the clear indication of the relationship that one item has to another. West, Farmer, and Wolff (1991) summarize nine types of cognitive relationships from the research:

Name	Relationship	Example
1. Classification	A is an example of B	A cat is a mammal.
2. Defining/subsuming	A is a property of B	Hair is a characteristic of a mammal.
3. Equivalence	A is identical to B	$2(a + b) = 2(b + a)$
4. Similarity	A is similar to B	A donkey is like a mule.
5. Difference	A is unlike B	A spider is not an insect.
6. Quantity	A is greater/less than B	A right angle is greater than an acute angle.
7. Time sequence	A occurs before/after B	In mitosis, prophase occurs before metaphase.
8. Causal	A causes B	Combustion produces heat.
9. Enabling	A enables/allows B	A person must be at least 18 years old to vote.

PRACTITIONER'S CORNER

Teaching to Both Hemispheres:
Concept Mapping – Continued

Below are three common types of concept maps. In each, the relationship between items is written as a legend (for a few types) or next to the line connecting the items (when there are many types).

• Spider maps illustrate classification, similarity, and difference relationships.

• Hierarchy maps illustrate defining and/or subsuming, equivalence, and quantity relationships.

• Chain maps illustrate time sequence, casual, and enabling relationships.

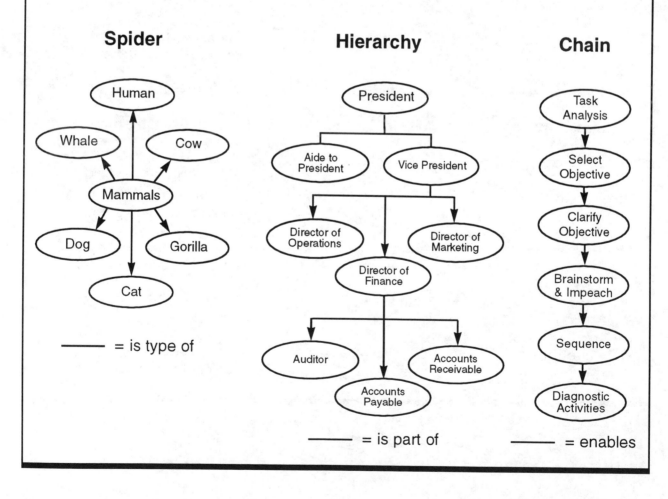

PRACTITIONER'S CORNER

Teaching to Both Hemispheres:
Concept Mapping – Continued

Below are three more types of concept maps.

• Story maps are useful for classifying main ideas with supporting events and information from the story.

• Analogy maps illustrate similarities and differences between new and familiar concepts.

• K-W-L maps illustrate degree of new learning for enabling.

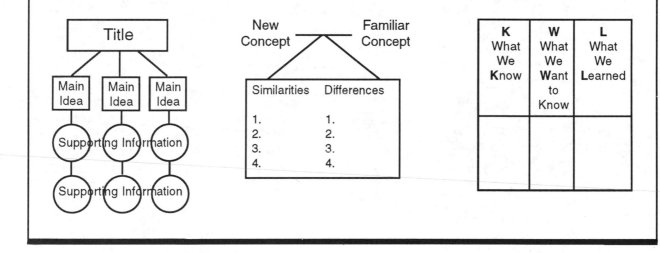

Story Map

Title

Main Idea | Main Idea | Main Idea

Supporting Information

Supporting Information

Analogy Map

New Concept — Familiar Concept

Similarities   Differences
1.   1.
2.   2.
3.   3.
4.   4.

K-W-L Map

K What We **K**now	W What We **W**ant to Know	L What We **L**earned

CHAPTER 6

THINKING SKILLS AND LEARNING

Sometimes memorization is important and useful. In general, however, teaching devoted to memorization does not facilitate the transfer of learning and probably interferes with the subsequent development of understanding. By ignoring the personal world of the learner, educators actually inhibit the effective functioning of the brain.

— Renate Caine and Geoffrey Caine,
Making Connections: Teaching and the Human Brain

Chapter Highlights. This chapter discusses some of the characteristics and dimensions of human thinking. It reviews Bloom's Taxonomy, notes its continuing compatibility with current research on higher-order thinking, and explains its relationship to difficulty, complexity, and intelligence.

The Thinking Brain

How can something as tangible as the human brain create such phantom things as ideas? How does it create Beethoven's symphonies, Michelangelo's sculptures, and Einstein's universe? What processes translate the countless neuron firings into thoughts, and then into products of magnificent beauty or weapons of destruction? The human brain collects information about the world and organizes it to form a representation of that world. This representation, or mental model, describes *thinking*, a process that an individual human uses to function in that world.

Characteristics of Human Thinking

Thinking is easier to describe than to define. Its characteristics include the daily routine of reasoning where one is at the moment, one's objective, and how to get there. It includes developing concepts, using words, solving problems, abstracting, intuiting, and anticipating the future. Other aspects of thinking include learning, memory, creativity, communication, logic, and generalization. How and when we use these aspects often determine the success or failure of our many interactions with our environment. This chapter discusses thinking, explores strategies that attempt to describe the characteristics of various types of thinking, and suggests how they can be used in the classroom to promote higher-order thinking and learning.

Types of Thinking

Answer these questions:

Who was the second president of the United States?

What are the similarities and differences between the post-Civil War and post-Vietnam War periods?

Defend why we should or should not have capital punishment.

Each of these questions requires you to think, but the type of thinking involved is not the same. The first question requires you to simply refer to a listing you have in long-term storage that recalls the sequence of presidents. Dealing with the second question is quite different. You must first recall what you have stored about both wars, separate these items into lists, then analyze them to determine which events were similar and which were different. The third question requires the retrieval and processing of large amounts of information about capital punishment, its impact on society, and its effectiveness as a deterrent to crime. Then you need to form a judgment about whether your representation of how certain people (criminals) will be influenced by a capital punishment penalty. These three questions require different and increasingly complex thought processes to arrive at acceptable answers. Thus, some thinking is more complex than other thinking.

The brain has evolved different mechanisms for dealing with various situations. Logic is one of those. It recognizes, for example, that if A is equal to B, and B is equal to C, then A must be equal to C. There are other mechanisms, too. Rationality, pattern identification, image making, and approximation are all forms of thinking that serve to help the individual deal with a concept, a problem, or a decision.

Thinking as a Representational System

While the file cabinets and their ordered system are useful metaphors for explaining the operation of long-term storage in the information processing model, they do not explain all the situations one encounters when the brain behaves as a representational system. Sometimes we cannot recognize a person's face, but we remember the name and the events that surrounded our first meeting with this person. As Restak (1988) notes, just thinking of the word *beach* evokes a complex series of mental events that corresponds to the internal representation we have of all the beaches we have ever encountered. Beaches gleam in the sun, are often hot, create a shoreline, merge with water, are dotted with umbrellas, and recall memories of holiday fun. The word itself is not actually a beach, but it brings forth many associations having to do with beaches. This is an example of a representational system and it illustrates the diversity of patterns in human thinking. It is this recognition of diversity that has led to the notion of multiple intelligences, that is, that an individual's thinking patterns vary when encountering different challenges, and that these semi-autonomous variations in thinking result in different degrees of success in learning.

Thinking and Emotion

Emotions play an important role in the thinking process. In Chapter 2 we discussed the amygdala that encodes emotional messages to long-term storage. We also noted that emotions often take precedence during cerebral processing and can impede or assist cognitive learning. If we like what we are learning, we are more likely to maintain interest and move to higher-level thinking. When we dislike the learning, we tend to spend the least amount of time with it and to stay at minimal levels of processing.

Can Thinking Be Taught?

This ordinary experience of thinking about a beach raises intriguing questions about how the brain is organized to think with increasing complexity. What skills does the human brain need to maneuver through simple and complex thoughts? Can these skills be learned and, if so, how and when should they be taught?

Perhaps a more basic question is: Can we teach people to think? Some educators believe the answer to this question is a resounding *yes*, and have published programs to teach thinking. These programs grew out of the realization during the past decade that students still do not think as critically as they should to be successful in a world that is constantly changing and increasingly complex. While I agree with this premise and admire their initiative, I believe their approach is somewhat misleading in light of what we know about the operations of the human brain. Their efforts to "teach thinking" advance the notion that young human beings do not think and thus must be taught. On the contrary, there is growing evidence that humans are born with a brain that has all the sensory components and neural organization necessary to survive successfully in its environment. The neural organization changes dramatically, of course, as the child grows and learns, resulting in the expansion of some networks and the elimination of others.

Even the most superficial look at human information processing reveals a vast system of magnificent neural networks that can learn language, recognize one face among thousands, and infer an outcome by rapidly analyzing data. Every bit of evidence available suggests that the human brain is *designed* for thinking. To imply that we must teach it to think demeans its structure and functions, ignores the current research, insults the natural curiosity of our students, and arrogantly suggests that if we did not do so, the individual would flounder in a "thoughtless" environment where survival would be the primary worry.[11]

Schools Demand Little Complex Thinking

I suggest that the reason our students are not thinking critically is that we have not exposed them to models or situations in school that require them to do so. Schooling, for the most part, demands little more than convergent thinking. Its practices and testing focus on content acquisition through rote rehearsal rather than the processes of thinking for analysis and synthesis. Too often, merely repeating the answer is considered thinking, rather than the process used to get the answer. Consequently, students and

> **We do not teach the brain to think. We can, however, help learners to organize content to facilitate more complex processing.**

teachers have become accustomed to dealing with learning at the lowest levels of complexity. What we are trying to do now is recognize these limitations, rewrite curricula, retrain teachers, and encourage students to use their innate thinking abilities to process learning at higher levels of complexity. In other words, we are teaching them *how to organize content in such a way that it facilitates and promotes higher-order thinking*, and not *teaching them to think*.

This distinction does not "split hairs" or "play with words." On the contrary, it is a very important distinction that determines the perspective we have when dealing with learners. Teachers who believe they are teaching students *how to think* perpetuate the teaching/learning scheme that treats students "as vessels to be filled." But accepting that we are *sharpening their skills to facilitate their thinking* places the teacher in the proper position of guiding students through the more effective use of their innate processes and abilities. The teacher's role shifts, as a current saying goes, from being the "sage on the stage" to the "guide on the side."

> **Test Question No. 11:** *People must be taught to do higher-order thinking.*
>
> **Answer:** *False. We begin thinking from birth (if not before). We can teach learners how to organize the content (such as using critical attributes and mnemonics) to promote more efficient thinking.*

---

11. Additional support for the concept that the human brain is genetically wired for learning and thinking can be found in G. Edelman, *Bright Air, Brilliant Fire: On the Matter of the Mind* (New York: Basic Books, 1992) and in M. Gazzaniga, *Nature's Mind* (New York: Basic Books, 1992).

The Dimensions of Human Thinking

Designing Models

Cognitive psychologists have been designing models for decades in an effort to describe the dimensions of thinking and the levels of complexity of human thought. The models have generally divided thought into two categories, convergent or lower-order thinking, and divergent or higher-order thinking. More recently, multi-dimensional frameworks, such as the *Dimensions of Thinking* project (Marzano et al., 1988), have appeared that attempt to describe all aspects of thinking in detail. Of course, a model is only as good as its potential for achieving a desired goal (in this case, encouraging higher-order thinking) and the likelihood that teachers feel sufficiently comfortable with it to make it a regular part of their classroom practice. In examining the models that describe the dimensions of thinking, most include the following four major areas:

1. **Basic Processes.** The tools we use to transform and evaluate information:

   Observing – includes recognizing and recalling.

   Finding patterns and generalizing – includes classifying, comparing and contrasting, and identifying relevant and irrelevant information.

   Forming conclusions based on patterns – includes hypothesizing, predicting, inferring, and applying.

   Assessing conclusions based on observations – includes checking consistency, identifying biases and stereotypes, identifying unstated assumptions, recognizing over and under-generalizations, and confirming conclusions with facts.

   The consistency with which these basic processes appear in most models results from the recognition that they allow us to make sense of our world by pulling together bits of information into understandable and coherent patterns. Further, these processes support the notion that conclusions should be based on evidence. From these conclusions, we form patterns that help us to hypothesize, infer, and predict.

2. **Domain-Specific Knowledge.** This refers to the knowledge in a particular content area that one must possess in order to carry out the basic processes described above.

3. **Metacognition.** The awareness one has of one's own thinking processes. It means that students should know when and why they are using the basic processes, and how they relate to the content they are learning.

4. **Affective Domain.** As mentioned earlier, researchers are more aware than ever of the role the affective domain (emotions and feelings) plays in learning, in this case, in the development and use of thinking skills. When students recognize the power of their own thinking, they use their skills more and solve problems for themselves rather than just waiting to be told the answers.

The question now is: What model can teachers use that, when properly implemented, promotes thinking, has been successful in the past, and holds the promise of success for the future? My response is to revisit the taxonomy of the cognitive domain developed over 40 years ago by Benjamin Bloom.

Revisiting Bloom's Taxonomy of the Cognitive Domain

Why This Model?

"Taste them again for the first time" says the announcer in a recent television commercial, hoping to entice viewers to resist the fad cereals and retry one that has been around for decades. In education, it seems often we are looking for the new quick fix to solve problems. I propose that a thinking skills model that has been around for decades may, like that cereal, be our answer to raising student thinking to higher levels.

One of the more enduring and useful models for enhancing thinking was developed by Benjamin Bloom in the 1950s. Bloom's system of classification, or taxonomy, identifies six levels of complexity of human thought. Reintroducing this in classes can upgrade the quality of teacher instruction and student learning for the following reasons:

- It is familiar to many prospective and practicing teachers.

- It is user-friendly and simple when compared to other models currently emerging.

- It requires only modest retraining for teachers to understand the relationship between the difficulty and complexity components.

- It helps teachers recognize the difference between difficulty and complexity, so they can help slower learners improve their thinking and achievement significantly.

- It can be implemented in every classroom immediately without waiting for major reform or restructuring.

- It is inexpensive in that teachers need only a few supplementary materials to use with the current curriculum.

- It motivates teachers since they see their students learning better, thinking more profoundly, and showing more interest.

I am very much aware that Bloom's Taxonomy has been standard fare in preservice and inservice teacher training for many years. Yet I suspect, as Bloom himself has conjectured, that the taxonomy's value as a model for moving all students to higher levels of thinking has barely been explored. In fact, my experience has been that most teachers remember this model with little enthusiasm and with even less understanding of its use to promote thinking and learning. More important, as we will discuss later, its connection to student ability has been largely misunderstood and misapplied. This situation is regrettable since the model is easy to understand and, when used correctly, can accelerate learning and elevate student interest and achievement, especially for slower learners.

The Model's Structure

Let's look at the model to understand how it organizes complexity and to appreciate its value in aiding less able students to experience the excitement of higher-order thinking and the exhilaration of greater achievement.

> **Bloom's Taxonomy remains one of the most useful tools for moving students, especially slower learners, to higher levels of thinking.**

The six levels of Bloom's Taxonomy (p. 117), from the least to the most complex, are: knowledge, comprehension, application, analysis, synthesis, and evaluation. While there are six separate levels, Bloom and others recently adopted the notions that the hierarchy of complexity is not rigid and that the individual may move easily among the levels during extended processing.

Below is a review of each level using the story of *Goldilocks* and the bombing of Pearl Harbor as examples of how two differing concepts can be taken through the taxonomy.

Knowledge

Knowledge is defined as the mere rote recall of previously learned material, from specific facts to a definition or a complete theory. All that is required is bringing it forth in the form it which it was learned. It represents the lowest level of learning in the cognitive domain since there is no presumption that the learner understands what is being recalled. Students in first grade recite the Pledge of Allegiance daily. Do they comprehend what they are saying? If so, would one fine, patriotic boy have started his pledge with, *I led the pigeons to the flag of the United States of America ...*?

Examples: What did Goldilocks do in the three bears' house?
            What was the date of the bombing of Pearl Harbor?

Comprehension

This level describes the ability to make sense of the material. This may occur by converting the material from one form to another (words to numbers), by interpreting the material (summarizing a story), or by estimating future trends (predicting consequences or effects). This learning goes beyond mere rote recall and represents the lowest level of understanding. When a student understands the material, rather than merely recalling it, the material becomes available for future use to solve problems and to make decisions. Comprehension questions attempt to determine if the students understand the information in a sensible way.

> Examples: Why did Goldilocks like the baby bear's things best?
> Why did the Japanese bomb Pearl Harbor?

Application

Application refers to the ability to use learned material in new situations with a minimum of direction. It includes the application of such things as rules, concepts, methods, and theories to solve problems. The learner uses convergent thinking to select, transfer, and apply data to complete a new task. Practice is essential at this level.

> Examples: If Goldilocks came to your house today, what things might she do?
> If you had been responsible for the defense of the Hawaiian Islands,
>   what preparation would you have made against an attack?

Analysis

Analysis is the ability to break material into its component parts so that its structure may be understood. It includes identifying parts, examining the relationships of the parts to each other and to the whole, and recognizing the organizational principles involved. The learner must be able to organize and reorganize information into categories. This is a higher level because the learner is aware of the thought process in use (metacognition) and understands both the content and structure of the material.

> Examples: What things in the Goldilocks story could have really happened?
> What lesson did our country learn from Pearl Harbor?

Synthesis

Synthesis refers to the ability to put parts together to form a plan that is new to the learner. It may involve the production of a unique communication (essay or speech), a plan of operations (research proposal), or a scheme for classifying information. This level stresses creativity, with major emphasis on forming *new* patterns or structures. This is the level where learners use divergent thinking to get an *Aha!* experience. It indicates that being creative requires a great deal of information, understanding, and application to produce a tangible product. Michelangelo could never have created the *David* or the *Pietà* without a thorough comprehension of human anatomy and types of marble, as well

Bloom's Taxonomy of the Cognitive Domain

Below are the levels in decreasing order of complexity with terms and sample activities that illustrate the thought processes involved at each level.

LEVEL	TERMS	SAMPLE ACTIVITIES
Evaluation	appraise assess criticize evaluate judge support	Which of the two main characters in the story would you prefer to have as a friend? Why? Is violence ever justified in correcting injustices? Why or why not? Which of the environments we've studied seems like the best place for you to live? Defend your answer.
Synthesis	compose create design formulate produce rearrange	Pretend you were a participant in the Boston Tea Party and write a diary entry that tells what happened. Rewrite *Red Riding Hood* as a news story. Design a different way of solving this problem. Formulate a hypothesis that might explain the results of these three experiments.
Analysis	analyze contrast deduce differentiate distinguish infer	Which events in the story are fantasy and which really happened? Compare and contrast the post-Civil War period with the post-Vietnam War period. Sort this collection of rocks into three categories. Which of these words are Latin derivatives and which are Greek?
Application	apply calculate demonstrate practice	Use each vocabulary word in a sentence. Calculate the area of our classroom. Think of three situations in which we would use this mathematics operation.
Comprehension	compare convert explain examples summarize	Summarize the paragraph in your own words. Why are symbols used on maps? Write a paragraph that explains the duties of the mayor. Give an example from the story that shows the main character was concerned about the success of others.
Knowledge	define list label locate recall	What is the definition of a verb? What is 6 x 4? What are three symbols found on maps? Where and when does the story take place? What are the three branches of government?

as the ability to use polishing compounds and tools with accuracy. His artistry comes from the mastery with which he used his knowledge and skill to carve magnificent pieces. Although most often associated with the arts, synthesis can occur in all areas of the curriculum.

Examples: Re-tell the story as if it were called *Goldilocks and the Three Fishes*.
Re-tell the story of Pearl Harbor assuming the United States' armed forces had been ready for the attack.

Evaluation

Evaluation is concerned with the ability to judge the value of material based on specific criteria. The learner may determine the criteria or be given them. The learner examines criteria from several categories and selects those that are the most relevant to the situation. Activities at this level almost always have multiple and equally acceptable solutions. This is the highest level of cognitive thought in this model because it contains elements of all the other levels, plus conscious judgments based on definite criteria. At this level, learners tend to consolidate their thinking and become more receptive to other points of view.

Examples: Do you think it was right for Goldilocks to go into the bears' house without having been invited? Why or why not?
Do you feel that the bombing of Pearl Harbor has any effect on Japanese-American relations today? Why or why not?

Important Characteristics of the Model

Two points need to be made here. First, these levels are cumulative, that is, each level above "knowledge" includes all those of lesser complexity. A learner cannot comprehend material without knowing it. Similarly, one cannot correctly apply a learning without comprehending it. Second, the lower three levels (knowledge, comprehension, and application) describe a *convergent* thinking process whereby the learner recalls and focuses what is known and comprehended to solve a problem through application. The upper three levels (analysis, synthesis, and evaluation) describe a *divergent* thinking process, since the learner's processing results in new insights and discoveries that were not part of the original information. When the learner is thinking at these upper levels, they flow naturally from one to the other and the boundaries disappear.

Testing Your Comprehension of the Taxonomy

To see if you comprehend the taxonomy's six different levels, complete the activity below. Then look at the answers and explanation following the activity.

Directions. Identify the highest level (remember, the levels are cumulative) of the taxonomy indicated in these learning objectives.

1. Given a ruler to measure the room, find how long the room is.
2. What is the Sixth Amendment to the U.S. Constitution?
3. Given copies of the Articles of Confederation and the Bill of Rights, the learner will write a comparison of the two documents and discuss similarities and differences.
4. Identify and write a question for each level of the taxonomy.
5. Use your own words to explain the moral at the end of the fable.
6. Given two ways to solve the problem, the learner will make a choice of which to use and give reasons.
7. Create your own fairy tale including all the characteristics of a fairy tale.

Answers:

1. *Application.* The learner must know the measuring system, comprehend the meaning of length, and use the ruler correctly.
2. *Knowledge.* The learner simply recalls that the Sixth Amendment deals with the rights of the accused.
3. *Analysis.* The learner must separate both documents into their component parts and compare and contrast them for relationships that describe their similarities and differences.
4. *Application.* The learner knows each level, comprehends its definition, then uses this information to write the question for each level.
5. *Comprehension.* The learner shows comprehension by explaining the fable's moral.
6. *Evaluation.* The learner chooses between two feasible options and explains the reasons for the choice.
7. *Synthesis.* Using characteristics of fairy tales, the learner creates a new one.

The Taxonomy and the Dimensions of Thinking

To what extent does Bloom's Taxonomy meet the four areas mentioned earlier that are included within most of the newer models describing the dimensions of thinking?

Basic Processes. The six levels of the taxonomy cover all the skills included under these processes. *Observing* is contained in the levels of knowledge and comprehension. *Finding patterns* and *generalizing* are skills in the levels of knowledge, comprehension, and analysis. *Forming conclusions based on patterns* is in analysis and synthesis. Finally, *assessing conclusions* is a characteristic of the taxonomy's evaluation level.

Domain-Specific Knowledge. This is the equivalent of Bloom's knowledge level.

Metacognition. This is the one area that is not explicitly cited in any one of the six levels. Nonetheless, when analyzing or discussing the rationale for selecting from among equally viable choices at the evaluation level, the learner has to reflect on the processes used to arrive at the selection and gather data to defend the choice. This self-awareness of the thinking process used is the essence of metacognition. The other components, such as having a respect for self-monitoring as a valued skill, a positive and personal attitude toward learning, and an attention to learning through introspection and practice, are very likely to result from the accurate, frequent, and systematic use of the taxonomy's upper levels.

The Affective Domain. Since we are making comparisons to Bloom's Taxonomy of the Cognitive Domain, it is apparent that there is no reference to affective processes. Thus, we need to look at the Taxonomy of the Affective Domain, developed by Krathwohl (1964) who, along with Bloom and Masia, recognized the power of this domain of learning. Not only do we want students to learn cognitive information and skills and how to apply them, we also want them to appreciate and value their use. Developing positive attitudes in students toward learning enhances interest, increases retention, and should be a major goal of every teacher.

As with the cognitive domain, each of the five levels of the affective domain taxonomy is a prerequisite to the successful performance of the next higher level. Within each level there is a range of attributes. The five levels are:

Receipt. At this level, the range of receiving is when learners progress from merely being aware of cognitive information, to receiving it, then to directing their attention to it even when they could be distracted.

Response. This level deals with the degree of the learner's willingness to respond to the cognitive strategies, ranging from acquiescence to cooperation to enthusiasm for learning the skill.

Value. This level ranges from the learner's believing in the worth of the skill, to choosing the new skill over a previous skill, to developing a strong commitment to it.

Organization. This level ranges from learners identifying the characteristics of the cognitive skill to their bringing together elements, characteristics, and other attributes into a coherent whole.

Characterization. The learners' use of the strategies has become habitual and they have incorporated them systematically into their philosophies of learning.

Pairing cognitive and affective taxonomies provides a strong foundation to move students toward higher-level thinking as a regular part of learning practice.

The Critical Difference Between Complexity and Difficulty

Complexity and difficulty describe completely different mental operations, but are often used synonymously. This error, resulting in the two factors being treated as one, limits the use of the taxonomy to enhance the thinking of all students. By recognizing how these concepts are different, the teacher can gain valuable insight into the connection between the taxonomy and student ability. *Complexity* describes the *thought process* that the brain uses to deal with information. In Bloom's Taxonomy (Figure 6.1), it can be described by any of the six words representing the six levels. The question *What is the capital of Rhode Island?* is at the knowledge level, while the question *Tell me in your own words what is meant by a state capital* is at the comprehension level. The second question is more *complex* than the first because it is at a higher level in Bloom's Taxonomy.

> **Regrettably, teachers are more likely to increase difficulty, rather than complexity, when attempting to raise student thinking.**

Difficulty, on the other hand, refers to the *amount of effort* that the learner must expend within a level of complexity to accomplish a learning objective. It is possible for a learning activity to become increasingly difficult without becoming more complex. For example, the question *Name the states of the Union* is at the knowledge level of complexity since it involves simple recall for most students. The question *Name the states of the Union and their capitals* is also at the knowledge level, but is more difficult than the prior question since it involves more effort to recall more information. Similarly, the question *Name the states and their capitals in order of their admission to the Union* is still at the knowledge level, but it is considerably more difficult than the first two.

These are examples of how a student can exert great effort to achieve a learning task while processing at the lowest level of thinking. When seeking to challenge students, classroom teachers are more likely (perhaps unwittingly) to increase difficulty rather than complexity as the challenge mode. This may be because they do not recognize the difference between these concepts or that they believe that difficulty is the method for achieving higher-order thinking (Figure 6.1).

Connecting Complexity and Difficulty to Ability

When teachers are asked whether complexity or difficulty is more closely linked to student ability, they more often choose complexity. Some explain their belief that only students of higher ability can carry out the processes indicated in analysis, synthesis, and evaluation. Others say that whenever they have tried to bring slower students up the taxonomy, the lesson got bogged down. Yet studies (Bloom, 1976) show that the real connection to ability is difficulty, not complexity.

The mistaken link between complexity and ability is the result of an unintended but very real self-fulfilling prophesy. Here's how it works. Teachers allot a certain amount of *time* for the class to learn a concept, usually based on how long they think it will take the *average* student to learn it (Figure 6.2). The fast learners learn the concept in less than the allotted time. During the remaining time, their brains often sort the concept's sublearnings into important and unimportant, that is, they select the critical attributes for storage and discard what they decide is unimportant. This explains why fast learners are usually fast retrievers: They have not cluttered their memory networks with trivia.

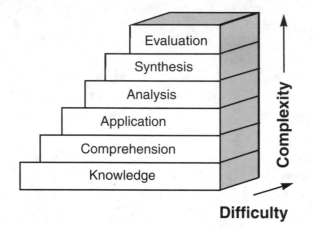

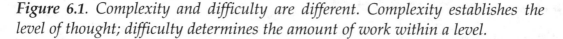

Figure 6.1. Complexity and difficulty are different. Complexity establishes the level of thought; difficulty determines the amount of work within a level.

Meanwhile, the slower learners need more than the allotted time to learn the concept. If that time is not given to them, not only do they lose part of the sublearnings, but they also do not have time to do any sorting. If the teacher attempts to move up the taxonomy, the fast learners have the concept's more important attributes in working memory to use appropriately and successfully at the higher levels of complexity. The slow learners, on the other hand, have not had time to sort, have cluttered their working memory with all the sublearnings (important and unimportant), and do not recognize the parts

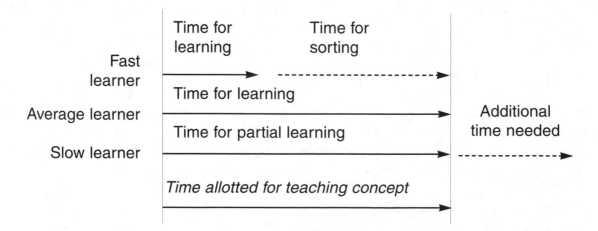

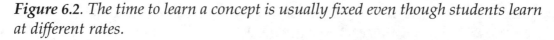

Figure 6.2. The time to learn a concept is usually fixed even though students learn at different rates.

needed for more complex processing. For them, it is like taking five big suitcases on an overnight trip, while the fast learners have taken just a small bag packed with the essentials. As a result, teachers become convinced that higher-order thinking is for the fast learners and that ability is linked to *complexity*.

> **With guidance and practice, slower learners can regularly reach the higher levels of Bloom's Taxonomy.**

The studies mentioned earlier included slower students for whom the unimportant material was not even taught. The curriculum was sorted from the start, and the focus was on critical attributes and other vital information. When the teacher moved up the taxonomy, these students in some cases demonstrated better achievement than the control groups! When teachers differentiate between complexity and difficulty, a new view of Bloom's Taxonomy emerges, one which promises more success for more students.

The Taxonomy and Constructivism

In their description of the characteristics of constructivist teachers, Brooks and Brooks (1993) note that these teachers ask open-ended questions and continually encourage students to analyze, synthesize, and evaluate. From this description, it seems evident that teachers who constantly use the upper levels of Bloom's Taxonomy are demonstrating, among other things, constructivist behaviors.

Curriculum Changes To Accommodate the Taxonomy

The implications from these studies are very significant in that they tell us two important things about using the taxonomy. First, if teachers avoid the self-fulfilling prophecy snare, they can get slower learners to do higher-order thinking successfully and often. Second, one way to accomplish this is to review the curriculum and remove the topics of least importance to gain the time needed for practice at the higher levels. An effective method for doing this is to set priorities among all the concepts in a curriculum, delete the least important bottom 25 percent, and use the time gained by this sorting and paring to move all students **up the taxonomy**. Finally, take advantage of the power of positive transfer by integrating these concepts with previously-taught material and connecting them to appropriate concepts in other curriculum areas.

> **Our students would make a quantum leap to higher-order thinking if every teacher in every classroom correctly and regularly used Bloom's Taxonomy.**

Other Thinking Skills Programs

There are other thinking skills programs and models available, and new ones are appearing regularly. My analysis of them is that they may be very useful after extensive teacher training, substantial curricular reform, and sizable investments for new materials. Until that happens, I urge that we implement the programs needed to train teachers now to use Bloom's Taxonomy correctly and successfully. I am convinced that if every teacher correctly implemented the taxonomy in every classroom and in every subject area, our students would make a quantum leap forward in their ability to do higher-order thinking. And they can do this now while waiting for more comprehensive reform efforts to become reality.

UP THE TAXONOMY!

PRACTITIONER'S CORNER

Some Tips on Using Bloom's Taxonomy

- **Watch the Behavior of the Learner.** The learner's behavior reveals the level of complexity where the learner's processing is taking place. Whenever the brain has the option of solving a problem at two levels of complexity, it generally chooses the less complex level. Teachers can inadvertently design activities that they believe are at one level of complexity that students actually accomplish at a different (usually lower) level.

- **Remember that the Levels are Cumulative.** Each level of the taxonomy includes the levels of lesser complexity. Therefore, ensure that the students have dealt with the new learnings thoroughly and successfully at the lower levels before moving to the upper levels. It is very difficult to create a product (synthesis) without a solid knowledge base and practice in applying the learnings.

- **Beware of Mimicry.** Sometimes students seem to be applying their learning to a new situation (application level) when they are just mimicking the teacher's behavior. Mimicry is knowledge level. For students to be really at the application level, they must understand why they are using a particular process to solve new problems.

- **Discuss Core Concepts at the Higher Levels.** Not all topics are suitable for processing at the upper levels. There are some areas where we do not want creativity (arithmetic, spelling, the rules of grammar), but teachers should consider taking to the upper levels every concept that they identify as a core learning. This helps students to attach meaning and make connections to past learnings, thereby significantly increasing retention.

- **Choose Complexity Over Difficulty for Most Assignments.** Remember that learners at all ability levels can do higher-order thinking. Give assignments that move students progressively up the taxonomy. Limit the exposure to trivial information and do not encourage students to spend time memorizing it, a process that many find monotonous and meaningless. Instead, give them divergent activities in analysis, synthesis, and evaluation that they will find more interesting and which are more likely to contribute to their deeper understanding of the learning objectives.

PRACTITIONER'S CORNER

Bloom's Taxonomy: Increasing Complexity

Examples become more complex from bottom to top and more difficult from left to right.

BLOOM'S LEVEL	INCREASING LEVEL OF DIFFICULTY ⟶	
EVALUATION	Compare the two main characters in the story. Which would you rather have as a friend and why?	Compare the four main characters in the story. Which would you rather have as a friend and why?
SYNTHESIS	Rewrite the story from the point of view of the dog.	Rewrite the story from the points of view of the dog and of the cat.
ANALYSIS	What were the similarities and differences between this story and the one we read about the Civil War hero?	What were the similarities and differences between this story, the one we read about the Civil War hero, and the one about the Great Depression?
APPLICATION	Think of another situation that could have caused the main character to behave that way.	Think of at least three other situations that could have caused the main character to behave that way.
COMPREHENSION	Write a paragraph that describes the childhood of any one of the main characters.	Write a paragraph that describes the childhood of each of the four main characters.
KNOWLEDGE	Name the major characters in this story.	Name the major characters and the four locations in the story.

(Left margin, reading bottom to top: INCREASING COMPLEXITY)

PRACTITIONER'S CORNER

Questions To Stimulate Higher-Order Thinking

Incorporate these questions into lesson plans to stimulate higher-order thinking. Be sure to read the guidelines for using Bloom's Taxonomy to ensure the maximum effectiveness of these questions. Remember to provide adequate wait time. Students should become accustomed to this type of questioning in every study assignment.

What would you have done?

What are some of the things you wondered about while this was happening?

What might happen next?

Why do think this is the best choice?

What do you think might happen if ... ?

What do you think caused this?

Can you predict what might happen in the future?

How is it like ... ?

How is it different from ... ?

Can you give an example?

Where could we go for help on this?

Could this ever happen?

Where do we go next?

Have we left out anything important?

Can we trust the source of this material?

In what other ways could this be done?

How many ways can you think of to use ... ?

Do you agree with this author/speaker? Why or why not?

Can you isolate the most important idea?

How would changing the sequence affect the outcome?

How could you modify this?

What details could you add to give a clearer picture?

How can you test this theory?

How can you tell the difference between ... and ... ?

CHAPTER 7

PUTTING IT ALL TOGETHER:
PLANNING FOR
TODAY AND TOMORROW

If we teach within and across the subject matters in ways that high-light powerful conceptual systems, we will have a "connected curriculum"—one that equips and empowers learners for the complex and challenging future they face.

— David Perkins,
Teaching and Learning for Understanding

Chapter Highlights. This chapter focuses on how to use the research presented to plan daily lessons. It suggests guidelines and a format for lesson design, and it mentions support systems to maintain the expertise in these techniques and move toward continuous growth.

The preceding chapters discussed some of the major strides that research is making in exploring how the brain processes information and learns. There are suggestions on how to translate these new discoveries into practical classroom strategies than can improve the efficacy of teaching and learning. But this information is of value to students only if teachers can incorporate it into their classroom practice so that it becomes part of their daily instructional behavior. The question now is: How do we use this large amount of information when planning our daily lessons?

Considerations for Daily Planning

General Guidelines

Start by keeping the following general thoughts in mind while planning:

- Learning engages the entire person (cognitive, affective, and psychomotor domains).

- The human brain seeks patterns in its search for meaning.

- Emotions are an integral part of learning, retention, and recall.

- Transfer always affects new learning.

- The brain's working memory has a limited capacity.

- Lecture results in the lowest degree of retention.

- Rehearsal is essential for retention.

- The brain is a parallel processor performing many functions simultaneously.

- Practice does not make perfect.

- Each brain is unique.

Lesson Design

To incorporate this research into daily planning, we need a lesson plan model as a framework. The widespread, successful model of lesson components that has evolved from Madeline Hunter's (1982) work at UCLA since the 1970s continues to serve that purpose well. I have made some minor modifications[12] to Hunter's original model to include some of the more recent strategies. The nine components of the design are:

1. *Anticipatory Set.* This strategy captures the students' focus. The set is most effective when it
   (a) allows students to remember an experience that will help them acquire the new learning (positive transfer)
   (b) involves active student participation
   (c) is relevant to the learning objective.

2. *Learning Objective.* This is a clear statement of *what* the students are expected to accomplish during the learning episode, including the levels of difficulty and complexity, and should include
   (a) a specific statement of the learning
   (b) the overt behavior that demonstrates whether the learning has occurred.

---

12. Hunter's original design had seven components. I have taken the *purpose of the lesson* from the *lesson objective* where Hunter placed it and made it a separate component to emphasize its importance in establishing the lesson's relevance for students. I have also added *closure* as a separate component because of the high impact this strategy has on improving retention of learning.

3. *Purpose.* This states *why* the students should accomplish the learning objective. Whenever possible, it should refer to how the new learning is related to prior and future learnings to facilitate positive transfer and meaning.

4. *Input.* This is the information and the procedures that students will need to accomplish the learning objective. It can take many forms, including reading, lecture, cooperative learning groups, audiovisual presentations, and so on.

5. *Modeling.* Clear and correct models help students make sense of the new learning and establish meaning. Models must be given first by the teacher and be accurate, unambiguous, and non-controversial.

6. *Check for Understanding.* This refers to the strategies the teacher will use during the learning episode to verify that the students are accomplishing the learning objective. The check could be in the form of oral discussion, written quiz, or any other overt format that yields the necessary data. After these checks, the teacher may provide more input, reteach, or move on.

7. *Guided Practice.* During this time, the student is applying the new learning in the presence of the teacher who provides immediate feedback on the accuracy of the learner's practice.

8. *Closure.* This is the time when the mind of the learner can summarize for itself its perception of what has been learned. The teacher gives specific directions for what the learner should mentally process and provides adequate time to accomplish it. This is usually the last opportunity the learner has to attach sense and meaning to the new learning, both of which are critical requirements for retention.

9. *Independent Practice.* After the teacher believes that the learners have accomplished the objective at the correct level of difficulty and complexity, students try the new learning on their own to enhance retention and develop fluency.

Important Note. Not every lesson needs every component. The teacher should choose the components that are relevant to the learning objective. The chart on p. 134 shows the lesson components, their purpose, their relationship to the research, and an example from a lesson on teaching the characteristics of suffixes.

Twenty Questions To Ask During Planning

Beginning on p. 135 are 20 questions that teachers should ask while planning lessons. The questions relate, of course, to information and strategies contained in previous chapters. After each question is the rationale for considering it and the chapter number where its main reference can be found.

Maintaining Skills for the Future

This book suggests many strategies that teachers can try to enhance the effectiveness of the teaching/learning process. The strategies have been derived from the current research on how we learn. Teachers who try these strategies for the first time may need support and feedback on the effectiveness of their implementation. The school-based support system is very important to maintaining teacher interest and commitment, especially if the new strategies don't produce the desired results in the classroom right away.

Building Principal's Role

Building principals play a vital role in establishing a school climate and culture that are receptive to new instructional strategies, and in maintaining the support systems necessary for continuing teacher development. Providing opportunities for teachers to master an expanded repertoire of research-based instructional techniques is an effective way for principals to foster collaboration and enhance the teaching staff's pursuit of professional inquiry.[12]

Types of Support Systems

Peer Coaching. This structure pairs two teachers who periodically observe each other in class. During the lesson, the observing teacher is looking for the use of a particular strategy or technique that was identified in a pre-observation conference. After the lesson, the observing teacher provides feedback on the results of the implementation of the strategy. The non-threatening and supportive nature of this peer relationship encourages teachers to take risks and try new techniques that they might otherwise avoid for fear of failure or administrative scrutiny. Peer coaches undergo initial training in how to set the observation goal at the preconference and on different methods for collecting information during the observation.

Study Groups. Forming small groups of teachers and administrators to study a particular topic further is an effective means of expanding understanding and methods of applying new strategies. The group members seek out new research on the topic and exchange and discuss information, data, and experiences in the group setting. Each group focuses on one or two topics, such as wait time, transfer, and retention techniques. Groups within a school or district can use jigsawing as a means of sharing information across groups.

Action Research. Conducting small research studies in a class or school can provide teachers with the validation they may need to incorporate new strategies permanently into their repertoire. For example, deliberately changing the length of the wait time after posing questions yields data on how the amount and quality of student responses vary

---

12. For more information on in-school support systems, see *Changing School Culture Through Staff Development*, edited by B. Joyce; Alexandria, Va.: Association for Supervision and Curriculum Development, 1990.

with the wait time. If several teachers carry out this research and exchange data, they will have the evidence to support the continued use of longer wait time as an effective strategy. This format also advances the notion that teachers should be involved in research projects as part of their professional growth.

Workshops on New Research. Periodic workshops that focus on new research findings in the teaching/learning process are valuable for updating teachers' knowledge base. Areas such as the transfer and transformation of learnings, reflection, and concept development are the targets of extensive research at this time and should be monitored to determine if new findings are appropriate for district and school workshops.

When educators encourage ongoing staff development activities, such as study groups and action research, they are recognizing that our understanding of the teaching/learning process is in continual change as the research yields more data on how the amazing brain learns. True professionals are committed to updating their knowledge base constantly, and they recognize individual professional development as a personal and lifelong responsibility that will enhance their effectiveness.

Conclusion

There are, of course, no magic answers that make the complex processes of teaching and learning successful all the time. Educators recognize that there are numerous variables that affect this dynamic interaction, many of which are beyond the teacher's influence or control. What teachers *can* control is their own behavior. My hope is that this book provides teachers with some new information, strategies, and insights that will increase their chances of success with more students.

LESSON COMPONENT	PURPOSE	RELATIONSHIP TO RESEARCH	EXAMPLE
Anticipatory Set	Focuses students on the learning objective.	Establishes relevance and encourages positive transfer during first prime time.	Think of what we learned yesterday about prefixes and be prepared to discuss them.
Learning Objective	Identifies what learning outcomes are to be accomplished by end of lesson.	Students know what they should learn and how they will know they have learned it.	Today we will learn about suffixes.
Purpose	Explains why it is important to accomplish this objective.	Knowing the purpose for learning something builds interest and establishes meaning.	Learning about suffixes will help us understand more vocabulary and give us greater creativity in our writing.
Input	Gives students the information and skills they need to accomplish the objective.	Bloom's **knowledge** level. Helps identify critical attributes.	Suffixes are letters placed at the ends of words to change their meanings.
Modeling	Shows the process or product of what students are learning.	Modeling enhances sense and meaning to help retention.	Examples are: -*less*, as in helpless; -*able*, as in drinkable; and -*ful*, as in doubtful.
Check for Understanding	Allows teachers to verify if students understand what they are learning.	Bloom's **comprehension** level.	John, tell me what you have learned so far about the meaning and use of suffixes.
Guided Practice	Allows students to try the new learning with teacher guidance.	Bloom's **application** level. Practice provides for fast learning.	Here is a list of 10 words. Add an appropriate suffix to each and explain their new meanings.
Closure	Allows students time to mentally summarize and internalize the new learning.	Last chance for attaching sense and meaning, thus improving retention.	I'll be quiet now while you think about the attributes and uses of suffixes.
Independent Practice	Students try new learning on their own to develop fluency.	This practice helps make the new learning permanent.	For homework, add suffixes to the words on page 121 to change their meanings.

QUESTION	RATIONALE	CHAPTER
1. What tactics am I using to help students attach meaning to the learning?	Meaning helps retention.	2
2. Have I divided the learning episode into mini-lessons of about 20 minutes each that don't exceed working memory's capacity?	Short lesson segments have proportionately less down-time than longer ones.	2
3. What motivation strategies am I using?	Motivation increases interest and accountability.	2
4. How will I verify if the students remember what they learned previously?	About 24 hours must pass to determine if what was previously learned is in long-term storage.	3
5. Which type of rehearsal should be used with this learning, and when?	Rote and elaborative rehearsal serve different purposes.	3
6. Am I using the prime-times to the best advantage?	Maximum retention occurs during the prime-times.	3
7. What will the students be doing during down-time?	Minimum retention occurs during down-time.	3
8. Am I using instructional modes from the learning pyramid that produce the greatest retention?	Different instructional modes result in different rates of retention.	3
9. Does my plan allow for enough wait time when asking questions?	Wait time is critical to allow for student recall to occur.	3
10. What chunking strategies are appropriate for this objective?	Chunking increases the number of items working memory can handle at one time.	3
11. What related prior learning should be included for distributed practice?	Distributed practice increases long-term retention.	3
12. How will I maximize positive transfer and minimize negative transfer?	Positive transfer assists learning; negative transfer interferes.	4
13. Have I identified the critical attributes of this concept?	Critical attributes help distinguish one concept from all others.	4

QUESTION	RATIONALE	CHAPTER
14. Are the concepts too similar to each other?	Concepts that are too similar should not be taught together.	4
15. How will I show students how they can use (transfer) this learning in the future?	The prospect of future transfer increases motivation and meaning.	4
16. Is it appropriate to use a metaphor with this objective?	Metaphors enhance transfer, hemispheric integration, and retention.	4
17. Have I included activities that are multi-sensory and engage both hemispheres?	Using many senses and both hemispheres increases retention.	5
18. Would a concept map help here?	Concept maps help hemispheric integration and retention.	5
19. How will I move this objective up Bloom's Taxonomy?	The taxonomy's upper levels involve higher-order thinking.	6
20. What emotions (affective domain) need to be considered or avoided in learning this objective?	Emotions play a key role in student acceptance and retention of learning.	6

GLOSSARY

Amygdala. The almond-shaped structure in the brain's limbic system that encodes emotional messages to long-term storage.

Axon. The neuron's long and unbranched fiber that carries impulses away from the cell to the next neuron.

Bloom's taxonomy of the cognitive domain. A model developed by Benjamin Bloom in the 1950s for classifying the complexity of human thought into six levels.

Brain stem. One of the three major parts of the brain, it receives sensory input and monitors vital functions such as heartbeat, body temperature, and digestion.

Cerebellum. One of the three major parts of the brain, it coordinates muscle movement.

Cerebrum. The largest of the three major parts of the brain, it controls sensory interpretation, thinking, and memory.

Chunking. The ability of the brain to perceive a coherent group of items as a single item or chunk.

Closure. The teaching strategy that allows learners quiet time in class to mentally reprocess what they have learned during a lesson.

Cognitive belief system. The unique construct one uses to interpret how the world works, based on experience.

Computerized axial tomography (CAT) scanner. An instrument that uses X-rays and computer processing to produce a detailed cross-section of brain structure.

Confabulation. The brain's replacement of a gap in long-term memory by a falsification which the individual believes to be correct.

Corpus callosum. The bridge of nerve fibers connecting the left and right cerebral hemispheres and allows communication between them.

Critical attribute. A characteristic that makes one concept different from all others.

Dendrite. The branched extension from the cell body of a neuron that receives impulses from nearby neurons through synaptic contacts.

Electroencephalograph (EEG). An instrument that charts fluctuations in the brain's electrical activity via electrodes attached to the scalp.

Engram. The permanent memory trace that results when brain tissue is anatomically altered by an experience.

Glia cells. Special "glue" cells in the brain that surround each neuron providing support, protection, and nourishment.

Hemisphericity. The notion that the two cerebral hemispheres are specialized and process information differently.

Hippocampus. A brain structure that compares new learning to past learning and encodes information from working memory to long-term storage.

Limbic system. The structures at the base of the cerebrum that control emotions.

Long-term storage. The areas of the cerebrum where memories are stored permanently.

Magnetic Resonance Imaging (MRI). An instrument that uses radio waves to disturb the alignment of the body's atoms in a magnetic field to produce computer-processed, high contrast images of internal structures.

Mnemonic. A word or phrase used as a device for remembering unrelated information, patterns, or rules.

Myelin. A fatty substance that surrounds and insulates a neuron's axon.

Neuron. The basic cell making up the brain and nervous system, consisting of a long fiber called an axon which transmits impulses, and many shorter fibers called dendrites which receive them.

Neurotransmitter. One of over 50 chemicals stored in axon sacs that transmit impulses from neuron to neuron across the synaptic gap.

Positron Emission Tomography (PET) scanner. An instrument that traces the metabolism of radioactively-tagged sugar in brain tissue producing a color image of cell activity.

Primacy-recency effect. The phenomenon whereby one tends to remember best that which comes first in a learning episode and second best that which comes last.

Rehearsal. The reprocessing of information in working memory.

Retention. The preservation of a learning in long-term storage in such a way that it can be identified and recalled quickly and accurately.

Reticular Activating System (RAS). The dense formation of neurons in the brain stem that channels sensory information through the perceptual register.

Self-concept. Our perception of who we are and how we fit into the world.

Short-term memory. A temporary memory where information is processed briefly and subconsciously, then either blocked or passed on to working memory.

Synapse. The microscopic gap between the axon of one neuron and the dendrite of another.

Transfer. The influence that past learning has on new learning and the degree to which the new learning will be useful in the learner's future.

Wait time. The period of teacher silence that follows the posing of a question before the first student is called to respond.

Working memory. The temporary memory where information is processed consciously.

BIBLIOGRAPHY

Alba, J. W., and Hasher, L. "Is Memory Schematic?" *Psychological Bulletin* 2 (1986): 203–231.

Armbruster, B. B., and Anderson, T. H. *Spatial Learning Strategies*. Orlando, Fla: Academic Press, 1984.

Berliner, D., and Casanova, U. *Putting Research to Work in Your School*. New York: Scholastic, 1993.

Berliner, D., and Pinero, U. C. "How Memory Works: Implications for Teachers." *Instructor* 94 (1985): 14–15.

Bloom, B. S. *Taxonomy of Educational Objectives (Cognitive Domain)*. New York: Longman, 1956.

————. *Human Characteristics and School Learning*. New York: McGraw-Hill, 1976.

Bloom, F. E., and Lazerson, A. *Brain, Mind, and Behavior*. 2d ed. New York: Freemand and Co., 1985.

Bradshaw, J., and Rogers, L. *The Evolution of Lateral Asymmetries, Language, Tool Use and Intellect*. San Diego, Calif.: Academic Press, 1993.

Brainerd, C. J. "On the Measurement of Storage and Retrieval Contributions to Memory Development." *Journal of Experimental Child Psychology* 1984: 37.

Brooks, J. G., and Brooks, M. G. *In Search of Understanding: The Case for Constructivist Classrooms*. Alexandria, Va.: Association for Supervision and Curriculum Development, 1993.

Brown, S. M., and Walberg, H. J. "Motivational Effects on Test Scores of Elementary Students." *Journal of Educational Research* January-February 1993: 133–136.

Buzan, T. *Use Both Sides of Your Brain*. New York: E. P. Dutton, 1983.

Caine, R., and Caine, G. *Making Connections: Teaching and the Human Brain*. Alexandria, Va.: Association for Supervision and Curriculum Development, 1991.

Corick, J. A. *The Human Brain: Mind and Matter*. New York: Arco Publishing, 1983.

Cresswell, J. L. "Implications of Right/Left Brain Research for Educators." *School Science and Mathematics* February 1988.

Crossett, B. "Using Both Halves of the Brain To Teach the Whole Child." *Social Education* April 1983.

Damasio, A. R., and Damasio, H. "Brain and Language." *Scientific American* September, 1992.

Danesi, M. "The Contribution of Neurolinguistics to Second and Foreign Language Theory and Practice." *System* 3 (1990): 373–96.

DellaNeve, C. "Brain-Compatible Learning Succeeds." *Educational Leadership* October 1985.

DuFour, R. P. *The Principal as Staff Developer.* Bloomington, Ind.: National Educational Service, 1991.

Dunn, K., and Dunn, R. "Dispelling Outmoded Beliefs About Student Learning." *Educational Leadership* 107 (1987): 55–61.

Estes, W. K. "Memory Storage and Retrieval Processes in Category Learning." *Journal of Experimental Psychology*: General 2 (1986): 155-175.

Facklam, M., and Facklam, H. *The Brain: Magnificent Mind Machine.* New York: Harcourt Brace Jovanovich, 1982.

Finke, R. A.; Ward, T. B.; and Smith, S. M. *Creative Cognition.* Cambridge, Mass.: The MIT Press, 1992.

Fogarty, R., and Bellanca, J. *Patterns for Thinking, Patterns for Transfer.* Palantine, Il.: Skylight Publishing, 1989.

Freidman, S. L.; Klivington, K. A.; and Peterson, R. W. *The Brain, Cognition, and Education.* New York: The Academic Press, 1986.

Gage, N. L. *The Scientific Basis of the Art of Teaching.* New York: Teachers College Press, 1978.

Gambrell, L. B. "The Occurrence of Think Time During Reading Comprehension Instruction." *Journal of Educational Research* 2 (1983): 77–80.

Gardner, H. *Frames of Mind: The Theory of Multiple Intelligences.* New York: Basic Books, Inc., 1983.

Gazzaniga, M. "Organization of the Human Brain." *Science* 245 (1989): 947–52.

Good, T., and Brophy, J. *Looking in Classrooms,* 5th ed. New York: Harper and Row, 1991.

Grady, M. P. *Teaching and Brain Research.* New York: Longman, 1984.

Graham, S., and Golan, S. "Motivational Influences on Cognition: Task Involvement, Ego Involvement, and Depth of Information Processing. *Journal of Educational Psychology* June 1991.

Gregorc, A. F. "Learning/Teaching Styles: Their Nature and Effects." *Student Learning Styles.* Reston, Va.: National Association of Secondary School Principals, 1979.

Gur, R. C. "Sex Differences in Regional Cerebral Glucose Metabolism During a Resting State." *Science* (1995): 528–531.

Harmin, M. *Inspiring Active Learning: A Handbook for Teachers.* Alexandria, Va.: Association for Supervision and Curriculum Development, 1994.

Hart, L. A. *Human Brain and Human Learning.* New York: Longman, 1983.

———. "A Response: All Thinking Paths Lead to the Brain." *Educational Leadership* May 1986.

Hayes, D. A. "Transfer." *Journal of Educational Research* 4 (1983).

The Healing Brain: A Scientific Reader. Edited by R. Ornstein and C. Swencionis. New York: The Guilford Press, 1990.

Hooper, J., and Terisi, D. *The 3-Pound Universe.* New York: Macmillan, 1986.

Hortin, J. A. "Research for Teachers on Visual Thinking To Solve Verbal Problems." *Journal of Education Technology System* 4 (1984-85).

Hosford, P., (ed.) *Using What We Know About Teaching,* Alexandria, Va.: Association for Supervision and Curriculum Development, 1984.

Hunter, M. C. *Mastery Teaching.* El Segundo, Calif.: T.I.P. Publications, 1982.

Johnson, V. R. "Concentrating on the Brain." *The Science Teacher,* March 1985.

Kauchak, D. P. and Eggen, P. D. *Learning and Teaching: Research-Based Methods.* 2d ed. Boston: Allyn and Bacon, 1993.

Key, N. *Research Methodologies for Whole-Brained Integration at the Secondary Level.* Report No. SP 037894. Pueblo, Colo: U.S. Government Document Service, 1991.

Kimura, D. "Sex Differences in the Brain." *Scientific American,* September 1992.

Krathwohl, D. R.; Bloom, B. S.; and Masia, B. B. *Taxonomy of Educational Objectives —The Classification of Educational Goals: Handbook II: Affective Domain.* New York: McKay, 1964.

Lazear, D. *Seven Ways of Knowing: Teaching for Multiple Intelligences.* Palantine, Il.: Skylight Publishing, 1991.

Letteri, C. A. "Teaching Students How To Learn." *Theory Into Practice* 24 (1985).

Levy, J. "The Evidence Strongly Disputes the Idea That Students Learn with Only One Side of the Brain." *Educational Leadership* January 1983.

———. "Right Brain, Left Brain: Fact and Fiction." *Psychology Today* May 1985.

Loftus, E., and Ketcham, K. *The Myth of Repressed Memory.* New York: St. Martin's Press, 1995.

Marzano, R. J., et al. *Dimensions of Thinking: A Framework for Curriculum and Instruction.* Alexandria, Va.: Association for Supervision and Curriculum Development, 1988.

McKean, K. "Of Two Minds: Selling the Right Brain." *Discover* April 1985.

Medin, D. "Comment on Memory Storage and Retrieval Processes in Category Learning." *Journal of Experimental Psychology*: General 4 (1986): 373-81.

Meer, J. "Remembrance of Things Lost." *Psychology Today* 14 (1986).

Nummela, R. M., and Rosengran, T. M. "What's Happening in Students' Brains May Redefine Teaching." *Educational Leadership* 8 (1986): 49–53.

Ornstein, R., and Thompson, R. F. *The Amazing Brain.* Boston: Houghton Mifflin, 1984.

Parrott, C. A. "Visual Imagery Training: Stimulating Utilization of Imaginal Processes." *Journal of Mental Imagery* 10 (1986): 47–64.

Perkins, D. N. "Educating for Insight." *Educational Leadership*, October 1991.

————."Teaching and Learning for Understanding." *NJEA Review*, October 1993.

Perkins, D. N., and Salomon, G. "Teaching for Transfer." *Educational Leadership*, September 1988.

Phillips, L. "Closure: The Fine Art of Making Learning Stick." *Instructor* 97 (1987): 36-38.

Phye, G. D. "Inductive Problem Solving: Schema Inducement and Memory-Based Transfer." *Journal of Educational Psychology* 82 (1990): 826–31.

Purkey, W. *Inviting School Success.* Belmont, Calif.: Wadsworth Publishing Co., 1978.

Restak, R. M. *The Mind.* New York: Bantam, 1988.

Riesenmy, M. R.; Mitchell, S.; and Hudgins, B. B. "Retention and Transfer of Children's Self–Directed Critical Thinking Skills." *Journal of Educational Research* September-October 1991.

Rose, S. *The Making of Memory.* New York: Doubleday, 1992.

Rowe, M. B. "Wait-Time and Rewards as Instructional Variables: Their Influence on Language, Logic, and Fate Control." *Journal of Research on Science Teaching* 2 (1974): 81-94.

Rowe, M. B. "Wait, Wait, Wait ... " *School Science and Mathematics* 78 (1978): 207-216.

Russell, P. *The Brain Book.* New York: E. P. Dutton, 1979.

Shannon, M., and Rice, D. R. "A Comparison of Hemispheric Preference Between High Ability and Low Ability Elementary Children." *Education Research Quarterly* 7 (1983): 7-15.

Shaywitz, B. A., Shaywitz, S. E., and Gore, J. C. "Sex Differences in the Functional Organization of the Brain for Language." *Nature* (1995): 607–613.

Silverstein, A., and Silverstein, V. *World of the Brain.* New York: William Morrow, 1986.

Sousa, D. A. "Helping Students Remember What You Teach." *Middle School Journal* May 1992.

Spencer, M. "Instructional Techniques for Increasing Student Achievement."*NASSP Bulletin* April 1988.

Sperry, R. W. "Cerebral Organization and Behavior." *Science* 133 (1991): 1749–57.

Squire, L. R. "Memory and Hippocampus: A Synthesis from Findings with Rats, Monkeys, and Humans." *Psychological Review* April 1992.

Stahl, R. J. "Cognitive Information Processes and Processing Within a Uniprocess Superstructure/Microstructure Framework: A Practical Information-Based Model." Unpublished manuscript, University of Arizona, Tucson, 1985.

Stein, H. "Visualized Notemaking: Left-Right Brain Theory Applied in the Classroom." *The Social Studies* July-August 1987.

Sternberg, R. J. *How We Can Teach Intelligence*. Philadelphia, Pa.: Research for Better Schools, 1983.

————. "Thinking Styles: Keys to Understanding Human Performance." *Phi Delta Kappan* January 1990.

Thomas, L. *The Medusa and the Snail*. New York: Viking Press, 1979.

Tobin, K. "The Role of Wait Time in Higher Cognitive Level Learning." *Review of Educational Research* 1 (1987): 69–95.

Toneleson, S. W. "The Importance of Teaching Self-Concept To Create a Healthy Psychosocial Environment for Learning." *Education* 102 (1981): 96–100.

Weinstein, C. E. "Training Students To Use Elaboration Learning Strategies." *Contemporary Educational Psychology* 7 (1982): 301–311.

West, C. K.; Farmer, J. A.; and Wolff, P. M. *Instructional Design: Implications from Cognitive Science*. Englewood Cliffs, N.J.: Prentice-Hall, 1991.

Winkles, J. "Achievement, Understanding and Transfer in a Learning Hierarchy." *American Educational Research Journal* 2 (1986).

Winograd, E., and Soloway, R. M. "On Forgetting the Locations of Things Stored in Special Places." *Journal of Experimental Psychology:* General 4 (1986): 366-72.

Wlodkowski, R. J., and Jaynes, J. *Eager To Learn*. San Francisco: Jossey-Bass, 1990.